Your time is limited, don't waste it living someone else's life.

— Steve Jobs

Also by Cathy Fiorello

Al Capone Had a Lovely Mother

$\mathcal{S}$tanding
at the
Edge of the Pool

Life, Love, Loss
and Never Learning to Swim

CATHY FIORELLO

Breezeway Books

ISBN: 978-1-62550-545-3

Library of Congress Control Number: 2018907939

For Jenna Rose,

who did learn to swim

Contents

STANDING AT THE EDGE OF THE POOL

Standing at the Edge of the Pool

When my granddaughter Leah asked me if I would be the subject of a college paper she was writing dealing with images of womanhood in her generation and mine, I agreed. She flew to San Francisco from her home in New York and we spent three intense days talking about my life, past and present. The question of regrets came up in our discussions. Looking back, I asked myself, was there a risk not taken that I now wish I had? A fear not overcome that I should have? I gave what I thought at the time was a shallow answer. I said I regretted that I had never learned to swim.

On further thought, I feel that answer has real depth. The question brought back visceral memories of standing at the edge of the pool, wishing I could jump in but not believing I would pop back up again like all the other kids. It brought back the longing I felt as I stood at the ocean's edge watching my older sisters and brothers frolic in the waves, believing that if I went under water, I would not float back up to the surface, as they did. It brought back all those times I dared not let go of my mother's hand. I now think of that fear of taking the plunge as a metaphor for how I've lived my life: the times I jumped in, the times I stepped back.

I was in my early twenties, recently out of college and saving every dollar I could spare for a dream trip to Europe, my first. My uncle died and left me the beneficiary of a life insurance policy, enough to finally take that trip. I spent months planning it, booking transportation on the French ocean liner *Liberte,* reserving hotels, signing on for tours of wonders I had only seen in books. I was going alone; I was going to do it my way. This was to be my breakout adventure. I would quit the writing job that had taken years to climb up to and put my career on hold.

While I was doing all that planning, I started dating a man who was an artist at Parents' magazine, where I worked as a writer. With passport in hand and a departure date set, I realized that I didn't want to leave him. I cancelled the trip. We married, and built a life around all that marriage entails— children, mortgage, college savings plans. Twenty years later, kids sent out into the world, mortgage paid, tuition-free, I saw Europe for the first time.

I had never thought of cancelling that first trip as a regret. There's no time for regrets when you're young. You set your life's course and you plunge into it without looking back. Then, suddenly, it's 50 years later, and you begin every day looking back at the things you didn't do, the paths you didn't take, and you wonder: Had I taken that trip so many years ago, and fallen in love with Paris then as I did so many years later, would I at some point have lived there? How different would my life be today? My husband Phil, who had his first European trip when he was a college student, says it changed his life. But here he is, in the same place I am.

About those kids. Phil and I disagreed on many things, but having children wasn't one of them. We both wanted them. When we knew we wouldn't have our own, we didn't hesitate to seek them through adoption. We knew we were setting out on a risky path to an uncertain future. Fifty years ago, people were more concerned with the pitfalls of adoption than with its rewards. We listened to the cautions of family and friends. Nothing we heard, no matter how dire, mattered more than our need to have a family. Trusting our instincts, we began what became a seven-month process that ended with a green-eyed baby girl being placed in my arms.

Leaving the Spence-Chapin Adoption Agency on the Upper East Side of Manhattan, I felt a queasy mixture of elation and apprehension. The infant in my arms was wide awake, green eyes staring up at me, taking the measure of the woman who stared back at her, both of us wondering, *What have we gotten ourselves into?*

Three years later, we repeated the process and were rewarded with a son. This time, we were seasoned parents; we had no doubt we were doing the right thing. At our first meeting, the infant I had just met grasped the neckline of my sweater and wouldn't let go. I knew this child was meant to be mine.

My granddaughter Leah's assignment was to choose a woman she admired and learn of her roles in society and how changing times have influenced those roles. I took my part in this assignment seriously and submerged into an unsettling reflective period. When I look back at my life, I see the things I didn't do; Leah sees only what I have done. She looks at my life as ground-breaking for its time, and in some ways it was. By going to college, I didn't fit the mold set for women of my generation. I had to overcome my mother's objections; she didn't think higher education would make me a better wife and mother, the path followed by most girls in that day. But even then, I knew I wanted more.

Nor did she approve when I went back to work after ten years of stay-at-home mothering. Again, I was going against the norms of my time. Working moms were frowned upon then because it was believed they neglected their children and demeaned their husbands by questioning their ability to provide for the family. I took the flack on both scores and began a second career. It was something I needed to do, not only for myself, but also for my children. I've never believed that martyrs make good mothers.

Returning to Leah's paper, she concludes, "My grandmother is a woman who has always kept her hand up." I would like to say that's true, but I would be lying. I should have had my hand up much more often than it was. Instead of just wishing things were better, I should have worked to make them better. Joan Didion said, "A writer is always ratting somebody out." I'm ratting myself out here.

4

When Leah asked if I would be the subject of her paper, I thought, what a treat it will be to spend time with a busy college student who wants to reminisce with her grandmother. I did not expect to sit again on the stoop of the Brooklyn brownstone where I was born, to fight again the epic battles with my mother to go to college, to live again the delights of places I love, and to suffer again the heartache of loved ones I've lost. Nor did I expect to come to terms with the times in my life when I didn't take the plunge; to ask myself, if I had jumped into the deep end of the pool all those years ago, would I have gone on to face life's challenges more boldly?

The Stoop

If home is where your history begins, then 410 Second Street in the Park Slope section of Brooklyn, New York, is where history began for me and my sisters and brothers. We were all born there. I was the fifth and youngest child. We were divided into two age groups, three older and two very much younger. Joe, Rose and Lou came first, born two years apart.

There was a seven-year gap before Eleanor and I arrived, also two years apart. I was born into one of the darkest years of the Great Depression. Life was a struggle for everyone around me, but I remember thriving in an environment of clearly defined responsibilities: first my schoolwork, then my chores, then my reward—pasting movie stars' pictures into a cherished scrapbook.

7

Our four-story brownstone, which my father owned, was one of a row of steadfast stone soldiers standing side by side, sheltering the Italian immigrant families scrambling to make a better life for their children. There was no space between them, no grass or trees in front. A patch of green in the back was our yard. Too small for play, it was where my mother's geraniums and hydrangeas bloomed in summer and my father's prized fig tree, wrapped in white canvas, glowed ghost-like during the dark winter months.

A stone stoop led to the first floor entrance. Beneath that, down two steps from the sidewalk, was the entrance to the cellar, where my father stoked the furnace with coal and my mother strung lines of rope from wall to wall with clusters of wooden clothespins at each end. This is where diapers and sheets were dried in inclement weather. Adjacent to the cellar entrance was an iron-gated area where the younger children played and babies were aired in their carriages, mothers checking on them from their living room windows. For the first seventeen years of my life, I ran up that stoop, through the double-doored vestibule, climbed the stairs to the second floor, and reached the safety of home.

The brownstone at 410 housed a large part of my mother's family. I had an aunt on every floor and another across the street. My maternal grandmother lived two blocks away, on Garfield Place. There were dozens of aunts and uncles and cousins. The doors were always open; a hungry child could find a seat at a table on any floor. Because our mothers had so much to do, the older children looked after the young, who weren't allowed to cross the street without holding the hand of an older sibling or cousin. If my mother found me on Aunt Louise's side of the street, she would ask sternly, "Who crossed you?"

I remember listening on summer mornings for the singsong proclamations of Andrew, the produce peddler, whose offerings determined what we would be eating that night. His lethargic old mare, hitched to a sagging wagon, clip-clopped through the spray-washed streets of our neighborhood every day. As he pulled into Second Street, one of us kids ran home and yelled up the stairwell, "Andrew's here!" Our mothers, still wearing their aprons, gathered around the wagon. I joined my cousins in a second ring behind them, hoping Andrew would toss in my direction that day's blemished peach or plum that he couldn't sell. If a vegetable was bargain-priced on a given day, all the aunts bought it. If it was broccoli, all four floors of 410 exuded its pungent odor as dinnertime approached—even the dumbwaiter, a ramshackle wooden car that rattled between floors in an enclosed shaft. Working it manually with a rope pulley, calling up to Aunt Grace and Aunt Betty, or down to Aunt Anna, my mother used it to send or receive whatever was needed at a moment's notice: a spool of thread, two aspirins, a bowl of soup for a sick child.

On Saturday mornings, Eleanor and I went food shopping on Fifth Avenue with our mother. We went from store to store buying its specialty—the grocer, the butcher, the bread bakery, the Italian provisions store. Our last stop was the live chicken market where we were greeted by a raucous flock of birds, squawking and fluttering across a feather-strewn floor. When my mother made her choice, she would say, "That one," pointing to the unfortunate bird that would be our Sunday dinner. Knowing it was as good as cooked, the chicken flapped wildly across the market floor, the ill-tempered butcher in pursuit, spewing profanities meant only for the ears of the hapless hen. When he caught her, with one expert twist, he broke her neck. With a triumphant grunt, he delivered the beheaded bird to my mother. On the way home, seeing how shaken I was, she'd assure me, "The chicken didn't feel anything."

I made my first friends at PS 77, the elementary school a block away from home. Until then, all my playmates were cousins; the environment I lived in had been intrinsically Italian. Though the Irish neighborhood started on Ninth Street, just a few blocks away physically, it was a world away ideologically. There was no intermingling of the adults; the children met in school. I socialized with my Irish friends at the soda shop or the library, not in our homes. Our mothers had nothing in common except a mutual mistrust of each other. Adding to my mother's displeasure at my going out of my ethnic zone, was the fact that I was star struck by my Irish friends. "What do you see in those skinny Irish girls?" she would huff. I envied their short skirts and long legs, their cream cheese and jelly sandwiches that didn't ooze tomato sauce. I wanted to be dressed in pastel-colored clothes that fit me, not the baggy browns that I wouldn't outgrow next year. I wanted to be as "American" as my blonde, blue-eyed classmates.

On Wednesday afternoons, I was released early from school and sent to Saint Francis Xavier Catholic church for religious instruction. It was the Irish church but my family worshipped there because it was closer to home than Our Lady of Peace, where the thunderous sermons of the Italian priests echoed in the eaves and dared parishioners not to be God-fearing when it was they the kids who went there were afraid of. The priests at St. Francis held hell over our heads with a twinkle in their eye. Everything, it seemed to me, was easier for the Irish, even the path to salvation.

At Sunday mass I would sit mesmerized by the lilting voices of the Irish ladies, tinged with more than a little touch of the green. Their vocal responses to the liturgy were always out-of-sync with the rest of the congregation, finishing at least two syllables ahead, and proud *of* it. No matter how hard I tried, I never finished on the same note they did.

We were prepared to receive our sacraments by an order of nuns whose discipline rivaled that of our mothers. In all areas of my life—home, school and church—discipline was on the curriculum. As I passed from one sphere of authority to another in the course of a day, so the responsibility to mold my mind and purify my soul was passed from mother to teachers to nuns.

For everyone at 410—mothers, fathers and children of all ages—the center of social life in the early days of the Depression was the front stoop. On steamy summer nights, this is where we sat and watched the search lights sweep across the sky. My mother said there were baskets at the end of those lights that swooped down and scooped up naughty children who were never seen again. I believed her. I know now that the lights came from a large revolving beacon atop the St. George Hotel and the hotel owners had no interest in children, naughty or good. When a jingling bell announced the arrival of the ice cream truck, we were treated to a two-cent lemon ice.

During the day, the stoop's five broad steps were the gathering place for me and my friends. We came together at the end of an afternoon's play—some kind, any kind of ball for the boys, skating and jumping rope for the girls. Unlike those same gentrified steps today, there were no decorative planters dripping ivy and geraniums at each end. There was no place for ornamental beauty, not in our lives, nor on our stoop. Our steps were for getting in and out of the house.

As dusk settled in, the boys put down their sticks and balls and joined the girls who scrunched together on the crowded steps to make room for them. We were all ready for supper, but supper wasn't ready for us. Mothers on all four floors were still working on the evening meal. Soups bubbled. Tomato sauce simmered. Tempting aromas drifted out the vestibule doors as tenants came out and came home, picking their way through the kids on the steps. A quiet child, I mostly listened to the lively chatter around me.

"I'll trade you two Joan Crawfords for one Ginger Rogers," my cousin Bessie offered Eileen, her Irish classmate who had crossed the border into the Italian neighborhood to study with her.

"Take it, Eileen, that's a good deal," Julia advised.

Tuning out on the movie stars because I had nothing to trade that day, I turned my attention to the boys who were tossing challenging questions at each other.

"Who's your hero?" Carmine asked.

"Pee Wee Reese!" Joey shouted. The other boys on the stoop, also ardent Dodgers fans, yelled out names of their favorite baseball players. They compared batting and earned-run averages with an accuracy that would have delighted their arithmetic teachers.

I didn't join in either the girls' or the boys' conversations. But Carmine's question about a hero started me thinking. *How would I answer that question?* Easy. *My Dad.*

Throughout my childhood, Dad was my hero. When my mother was mad at me, he wasn't. When people exclaimed over Eleanor's red hair, he'd say, "Cathy can spell anything." And wasn't it he who rescued me when I lost the money for the class trip to the Bronx Zoo? He replaced it and never told my mother I had lost it. *Now, that's what I call a hero!* I wanted to shout to the kids around me.

"If you could do anything, anything at all, what would it be?" Sonny asked the other boys on the stoop. He gave his own answer first: "I'd knock in the winning run in the bottom of the ninth and clinch the pennant for the Dodgers."

I listened to the boys' declarations of bravado, then, speaking only to myself, I gave my answer to his question: *I'd win the all-school spelling bee for my father.*

I did.

This Miniature Immigrant

My father left Italy in 1908 and embarked on a voyage into the unknown. He was ten years old, his only travel companion was his eight-year-old brother. Being the older, my father was in charge, as he would be the rest of his life: in charge of his family, in charge of his business, in charge of any situation that required a cool head and a stout heart. It all began on Ellis Island.

It didn't begin well. For their own safety, unescorted children were detained until a relative or friend of the family came for them. My grandmother, whose husband had gone to Venezuela to seek his fortune and never returned, was left with four young children to raise: my father, the eldest, his brother, and two younger sisters. Rather than raise her children in the extreme poverty of Italy, she risked sending her boys to America alone, hoping they would establish a better life there, then send for her and the girls. Too young to understand the gravity of this journey, my father did what he was told and carried out his mother's desperate plan.

My grandmother arranged for the children to be met at Ellis Island and had sent money ahead to a friend who would sponsor them, but he never came. After a harrowing journey across a turbulent ocean on a ship packed with seasick immigrants and the barest facilities to meet their needs, the boys were sent to the detention area to await deportation, dashing all hopes for a new life in America. They were there for seven days. They slept on bunks against the wall, sat on benches along rough-hewn planks that served as tables, and ate from crude wooden bowls. Luckily for my family, no ship booked for a return trip to Italy arrived during that time. Finally, a kindly immigration officer took pity on the boys. "Is there someone we can notify?" he asked. My father had the name and address of a *paisano* who had emigrated earlier. The officer, using his own money for the postcard, sent a note describing the plight of the children, and they were rescued. They were allowed to leave Ellis Island and set out in search of the American dream. The Lady in the Harbor, who my father revered the rest of his life, had not turned her back on him.

The friend who took the boys off Ellis Island couldn't afford to keep them. He brought them to a Catholic orphanage, where they were fed and sheltered and, most important for their prospects in America, taught to read and write English.

They weren't at the orphanage long when a young couple of means came to adopt a child. My father and uncle were scrubbed and combed and displayed before them. Just one would be chosen for a privileged life in this new land. They chose my uncle. Now separated even from his brother, my father lived at the orphanage until he was twelve, when he was released to find work and support himself. Starting with the menial jobs a boy could get, over time he worked his way up to become a foreman at the American Can Company, which offered a secure job for as long as he wished to stay. But he had always wanted a business of his own, to be the architect of his own destiny after so many years of having others set his course. In 1928, he got his big chance. He left the security of American Can and bought a small soft drinks factory. In 1929, the economy crashed and he, along with the rest of the country, was plunged into the long, dark years of the Depression. He was married and the father of four, with a fifth on the way, and though my mother rued the day he left American Can, he never did. He loved having his own shop, floundering though it was, and he hung on until things got better, then built the business again. It was so much a part of who he was that we kids used to say, "If you prick Dad's finger, you'll get ginger ale."

As an adult, he found and reunited with his brother, and Uncle Tony, Aunt Victoria, and their daughter Yola joined our family circle. As soon as he could afford to, he brought his mother and sisters to America, too. At journey's end, he had accomplished everything his mother sent him to America to do. The story of that journey is an integral part of our family history. We all heard it from our father, we've all told it to our children. But none of us had understood the enormity of our father's immigrant experience until we, too, went to Ellis Island and retraced his first steps in the New World.

On a brisk fall day in 1992, all my siblings but Rose, who had succumbed to cancer at age 67, boarded a ferry at Battery Park in Lower Manhattan and sailed past the Statue of Liberty, disembarking at the eloquently restored Ellis Island Museum. For more than thirty years, Ellis Island was the Gateway to America. More Italians came through that immigration center than any other nationality. My father was one of them.

We had all eagerly contributed to the one hundred dollars it cost to have our father's name put on the Immigrant Wall of Honor, erected to commemorate the millions of immigrants who had built America "with their backs and their brains." When we found our father's name, we each ran a finger lovingly across the etched *Joseph Ferrise*. We felt he was there with us, this man whose awed proclamations of "Only in America!" rang in our ears throughout our childhood, and in our hearts on this emotional day.

The most moving part of the tour for us was the detention area. As we huddled in this bleak, narrow room, with triple-tiered bunk beds against the walls, and tables set as they had been when masses of hopeful immigrants passed through, we knew without a doubt that we were standing where our father had stood before us. I had an overwhelming sense of this miniature immigrant, one arm clasping his few possessions, the other around his even smaller brother. Had he slept on one of these bunks, I wondered, eaten from one of these bowls? As I stood in painful awe, trying to hold back tears of my own, I heard a sob behind me. It was my brother Joe, the oldest of the five children, the closest to my father, the one who had understood him best. He, too, was overcome with the drama of the child whose second chance in life had started here, in hardship and fear of the unknown; who had gone on to become the gentle, steadfast father who guided us through childhood, preparing us for a life he had dared not dream of for himself.

Summering With Aunt Anna

Growing up in a Brooklyn brownstone during the Depression, I was surrounded by characters who could challenge Damon Runyon's stable of lovable oddballs. In my case, they were called family. Each of us had our own way of dealing with adversity. My Aunt Anna never let the hard times affect her zest for life.

For the rest of us, life was a serious matter. I had my mandated duties: school work and chores, in that order, which I had to perform before I earned the privilege of play. It never occurred to me to shirk my responsibilities. They were a fact of my life, drilled into me by a mother who tolerated no deviation from the rules.

Aunt Anna must have missed that lesson when she was growing up. The youngest of my mother's five sisters, she lived her life with a panache that thumbed its nose at the economic disaster that had descended on all of us. She was full of fun at a time when there was nothing to laugh about. Vivacious and shapely, she was the only sister who was fashion-conscious. At a time when it was a struggle to buy a cloth coat, she had a fur stole that she flung around her shoulders letting the pointed head and tiny feet of the fox whose skin she was wearing decide where to land; wherever that was, she looked smart. I was in awe of that fox. "Can I touch it?" I'd ask. I'd run my hand quickly across the feet not daring to touch the head, whose menacing black eyes glared back at me. My mother had nothing as stylish. She had five children to cook for; when I think of her, she's always wearing an apron.

I never remember Aunt Anna being alone. She was always in a crowd, and always at its center. Because of her flamboyant behavior, she was often at the center of family discord, too. She was the only woman in the family who smoked, the only mother who went to the movies in the afternoon. Baseball was her passion; she was an ardent Brooklyn Dodgers fan. When the team was on home turf at Ebbets Field, so was Aunt Anna. She was at once a bane and a boon to her sisters, who swung from outrage at her antics to joy in having her around. "You should be ashamed of yourself," my straitlaced Aunt Grace would tell her. Aunt Anna never was. She would throw her arms around her chastising sister and all was forgiven. Too young to care about her indiscretions, I loved the excitement that entered a room with this fun-loving aunt. How much more drab those times would have been without her.

Strangely enough, my no-nonsense disciplinarian mother had a close relationship with this sister who lived life on the wild side. We rented a house in Greenwood Lake, New York, with Aunt Anna's family in the summer. My father and Uncle Joe, her husband, joined us on weekends. They weren't the only ones. Summering with Aunt Anna was never the respite from city stress that my mother had envisioned. On Friday afternoons, a carload of her sister's friends swerved into our driveway, horn honking, radio blaring, gravel flying. Aunt Anna, who minutes before had been lying in bed with one of her legendary headaches, sprang to life—the weekend's entertainment had arrived. Among the regulars were Tommy Patcheye, who no longer wore the patch but couldn't shed the nickname; Charlie, the Wall Streeter, who dressed for the Stock Exchange even at the lake; Slim, the barber, whose midlife paunch belied the name he was stuck with.

Eleanor and I and Aunt Anna's son Junior stormed the car, collecting hugs and gifts of candy and games we would play on the porch on rainy days. My father and Uncle Joe made emergency runs to the general store to accommodate the care and feeding of the new arrivals. Once settled in, Tommy, Charlie and Slim took us boating on the lake while my mother and Aunt Anna prepared a country feast for their city guests. They shucked corn and sliced tomatoes and cucumbers that were harvested that morning, a far cry from the wilting produce that Andrew the peddler delivered to their door at home. After dinner, my father drove us to the village sweet shop for a treat. My favorite was Charlotte Russe, cake in a paper cup with whipped cream and half a cherry on top. You ate it by pushing up the bottom of the cup.

When daylight ended, the music began, drowning out the night song of the cicadas. Candles that were lit to ward off mosquitoes cast a campfire-like glow on the dancers. Aunt Anna's signature bumps and grinds, unabashedly flirtatious, delighted her friends and embarrassed my mother. We kids watched the dancing from the porch where makeshift beds had been set up for us to make room in the house for the guests. We loved staying up late, telling ghost stories and catching the fireflies that swarmed above us. We had contests to see who caught the most. Eleanor always won. Nobody asked how many I had. I didn't like bugs and ran around pretending to catch them while secretly shooing them away. You had to be a really dumb firefly to land in my jar. It didn't matter; though we had punched holes in the lids of the jars we collected them in, they were all dead by morning.

I was always sad to see the Monday morning exodus of the weekend revelers, but I knew they would be back on Friday and the fun would begin again. My mother, who did most of the cooking and all of the cleanup after the partying, returned from those vacations in need of another.

Like a candle that burns brightest and flickers out soonest, Aunt Anna was the first of the sisters to leave us. She succumbed to cancer in her early sixties, surrounded by her sisters, all of them older than she. They lived on into their seventies. Aunt Grace, the sickly sister, outlived them all; she called it quits at 104.

Now, at reunions of the cousins who began life in that Brooklyn brownstone, Aunt Anna is a main character in the stories we tell. We remember the aunt who made the dark times brighter for all of us.

The French Ladies

I was eleven years old when the Japanese attacked Pearl Harbor on December 7, 1941, a day that will "live in infamy," and in my memory as one of those dates you never forget. My parents had been out for their Sunday drive and heard the news on the car radio. They made an immediate U-turn and came home. I heard my mother crying as she climbed the stairs to our second floor flat. "Why are you crying?" I asked. "My sons are going to war," she replied. She was right; my two brothers did go to war.

Though the United States had resolved to stay out of the conflict that was raging in Europe, an immediate declaration of war was made after the attack and we plunged, fully committed, into World War II. For the next four years, our country's being at war affected every aspect of my life. Unlike today's wars, it wasn't only the soldiers on the battlefields who fought World War II; they had the steadfast support of the men, women and children on the home front. We had their back; we were proud to do our part in what we all considered an honorable war. Unless they are in the family of servicemen deployed in Afghanistan, Iraq and other military bases around the world, today's schoolchildren go through the day without giving a thought to or making a sacrifice for the wars we are engulfed in. Patriotism does not drive their young lives.

My war, on the other hand, began with a betrayal that had to be avenged. Every year it was fought, we knew it was getting closer to the end, and that end would be victory. During that war, I lived a palpable patriotism every day—at home, where I adhered to food rationing restrictions, and at school, where I attended weekly assemblies that began with the Pledge of Allegiance and ended with a rousing rendition of Irving Berlin's *Over There*, a musical assurance that our boys would get the job done. Even at the movies, where RKO Pathé newsreels showing actual fighting on two fronts preceded feature films whose fictional war stories sent me out of the theatre hating the Japs and the Nazis. And in church, where every Sunday I prayed for the souls of the boys who were lost defending our country, and received Holy Communion with the safe return of my brothers as my special intention. Doing my part to help the war effort was woven into the fabric of my life.

When PS 77 sponsored a War Bond drive that would reward the seller of the most bonds with a Certificate of Honor, Eleanor and I threw ourselves into the drive; we wanted that certificate.

Bonds were one way the government financed the war. The most affordable one was an $18.75 investment in victory which matured over 10 years, with a final payout of $25. They were one of the most popular ways to participate in the war effort. We canvassed both sides of Second Street, knocking on the doors of relatives and neighbors. As part of our presentation we made a poster featuring "Uncle Sam," the ultimate symbol of patriotism, wearing a red, white and blue top hat, his index finger pointing fiercely at the viewer, asking, "What have YOU done for the War Effort today?" It was almost treason not to answer his call and many of our neighbors proved their patriotism by signing up for a bond.

With no space between the brownstones, there were a lot of doors on Second Street, and we had covered all of them when Eleanor decided to double back and try the door we had deliberately bypassed because my mother had told us not to knock on it, and we were certain it would not open for us if we did. It was on Aunt Louise's side of the street, in the middle of the block. Two elderly women lived there; nobody knew their history or their name, but rumor had it they were French and we believed it, thus they were labeled for all time as "The French Ladies." Rumor also had it they didn't like children. We kids believed that, too, and never played stick ball or jumped rope in front of their house. We didn't think of them as a spooky threat, like Boo in *To Kill A Mockingbird*. We weren't afraid of them. Our mothers ordered us not to bother them, and we didn't. They didn't socialize with the other people on the block. They were hardly ever seen leaving their house. They must have made grocery runs, but one thing we knew for sure—they didn't answer Andrew's raucous call; they never joined the women in their aprons at his produce wagon. They were considered unapproachable because, if there was such a thing as class on Second Street, the French Ladies were definitely on the upper tier.

But Eleanor left no stone unturned when it came to finding ways to get into trouble. "Mom said not to," I urgently reminded her, to no avail, as she boldly knocked on the forbidden door. I took my usual stance behind her, using her as a shield. She stood her ground, ready to take the consequences for both of us, whatever they would be. The door creaked open; in my mind it sounded like the opening of a crypt in a horror movie. I closed my eyes. Then I heard a lilting voice call out, "Who's there, Lily?" Lily replied, "Come quickly, it's the two young girls who live across the street." I opened my eyes and saw two women wearing long grey dresses with lace collars who were smiling and inviting us into their home. Eleanor, poster in hand, marched right in; I stood transfixed, my feet stuck to the top step of the stoop, until she came back and dragged me in by the sleeve of my coat.

Lily ushered us into the living room, which I remember as dark, but not threatening. Then she went into the kitchen, saying as she left, "Please wait for me to return before you tell us why you're here." The other sister, who never spoke, seated us on chairs that looked like thrones. They had high wooden backs, fancy carvings on the arms and a sculpted foot at the end of their two front legs. I had never seen anything like them. I didn't know I was sitting on a valuable antique; the chair just looked old to me. The rest of the room was similarly furnished, with marble-topped tables and couches that looked like nobody sat on them. Nothing in the room looked comfortable.

Lily returned with a tray bearing porcelain cups of steaming cocoa and a plate of cookies that looked too fancy to eat. She settled into a chair and turned to Eleanor. "Now, tell us why you're visiting us today," she asked. Holding up her poster, Eleanor went into the sales pitch that she had delivered up and down both sides of the street, an emotional appeal to help our boys overseas who were fighting to keep us safe. When Lily turned to me, I said, "We want to win the certificate at school for selling the most war bonds."

"Well, isn't that a patriotic thing to do," she said. "Your mother must be so proud of you."

All I could think was, *We're in big trouble when Mom finds out we were here.* Lily asked for two enrollment forms, then filled them out. She signed one and her sister signed the other. Eleanor and I were so excited—we didn't expect to sell one bond at this door and here we were, selling two! On Monday, when all the kids turned in the results of their weekend canvassing and the sales were tallied, Eleanor and I won the drive by two.

Eleanor maintained a friendship with the French Ladies over the years and, through visits to their home, she developed an appreciation for antiques. When she married, they gave her a unique gift. They told her to choose any piece of furniture in their living room as a wedding present. She picked a marble-topped hutch with two mirrored doors. That hutch, highly polished and lovingly cared for, occupied a prominent place in Eleanor's living room for as long as she lived.

The Forbidden Facts of Female Life

In my family, nobody went through puberty. It simply was not discussed. Therefore, nobody was prepared for it. When my period made its first frightening appearance, my sister Rose stepped in and introduced me to that basic fact of female life. My Aunt Louise made a special trip across the street to hug me and whisper in my ear, "Today you are a woman." I was eleven years old. I didn't feel any different from the kid I was yesterday.

Buying Kotex in those days when sex was in the dark was a sensitive issue. Since stores were not self-service then, you had to ask the sales clerk for them, so you waited until a woman was behind the counter. One of life's great embarrassments was having to ask a man for a box of your monthly needs, which were always stored out of sight. It still puzzles me that this essential rite of passage in a young girl's life was shrouded in an aura of shame and secrecy. This was true even at home, where my mother told her girls that we were not to leave evidence of our "time of month" where our brothers would see it. Not wanting to be embarrassed, we all kept the secret— from our brothers at home, from the boys at school, from men in general.

That's why, when I was just a kid, before I became a woman, I was often sent to the drug store by older sisters and cousins who didn't want to risk dealing with a male clerk. Not knowing what I was buying, and not yet indoctrinated in the shame of my sex, I skipped to the corner drug store, plopped a quarter on the counter and, following the explicit instructions I had been given, announced to all within earshot, "I would like a box of sanitary napkins, please." Then I took my two-cent reward for going to the store to the candy counter, where I bought a chunky chocolate bar with raisins and nuts and ate it on the way home.

Our sex education, such as it was, was filled with "don'ts." We were told what *not* to do with boys, but nobody told us *why*. Even when my cousin Annie got pregnant in her teens, nobody said the word. Her mother took to her bed. The adults whispered when we were around and not a word of explanation was offered to the children, who wondered why everyone was so upset. My young cousin was whisked away and married to a man she would not have chosen as an adult, the only acceptable option for a pregnancy outside of marriage at the time. Abortion, a crime and a sin, came with the risk of physical death or the death of a Catholic soul. Such dire consequences, yet pregnancy was a taboo subject. Neither our mothers nor our teachers, and certainly not our nuns, offered guidance against the pitfall that ruined my cousin's life.

Getting my first bra was another rite of passage for which my mother set the standard. Her rule for her daughters was no bras before the age of twelve. It was embarrassingly apparent that I was ready for one at eleven. When I asked for a bra my mother said firmly, "Not yet, you'll get one next year," and, like all her decisions, it was final. Eleanor came to my rescue. We locked ourselves in the bathroom and she cut an undershirt into what was a prototype for what was later known as a training bra. She knew just how to do it; she had made one for herself before my mother said yes to a bra for her.

Over The Rainbow

"Now remember," my mother said as Eleanor and I were leaving the house that morning. "Don't come home after school, go straight to Grandma's. I'll be there." I didn't know then, but that was the beginning of the end of my grandmother's life.

She was old, yes, but she had always been old to me. I never could imagine my grandmother as a young woman. There were no pictures of her early years. For the entire time I knew her, she had dressed all in black, mourning her husband's death until her own. He died in the Spanish Influenza epidemic before I was born, but I knew exactly what he looked like. His picture, a sepia-tinged black and white photo framed in a weather-beaten oval, was on his headstone in St. John's cemetery. He looked very strict. His hair was all white, but his mustache, extending beyond both ends of his stern mouth, was black.

One of our Sunday drive excursions was to St. John's to say a prayer at Grandpa's grave. First, we'd pick up Grandma, then, all settled in the car—Eleanor up front with my father, I tucked tightly between my mother and grandmother on the back seat—we headed for the Long Island Expressway which would take us to the cemetery. When we arrived, Eleanor and I would race between the aisles of graves to see who would find Grandpa's first. If we'd brought flowers, which we always did on his birthday and Fathers' Day, my father would clear the grave site of debris while Eleanor and I went to the pump to fill a container of water for the new plantings. Then we knelt in the grass and everyone whispered prayers for Grandpa's soul. Except Grandma; she just stood there and talked out loud to him in Italian, gesturing and shaking her head as if he were standing before her. Though Eleanor and I had never met him, our grandfather was very much a part of our young lives.

When we got to my Grandmother's house that afternoon, my mother met us at the door, a finger at her lips, telling us to hush so we wouldn't disturb Grandma. We were led to the spare room and told to do our homework, quietly. My mother spent the rest of the afternoon tending to her mother. Eleanor and I didn't know what was happening, but we knew it wasn't good. We knew the joy of life beginning as new babies came into our family, but we were shielded from the harsh realities that end a life. With our homework done and hours to go before we would be home, we did our best to entertain ourselves. At our Friday night movie that week, we had seen "The Wizard of Oz" and were entranced with Judy Garland as a character our age living this magical adventure. We couldn't get the music out of our head; we used it to veil the occasional moan that came from Grandma's room, singing "Over the Rainbow," again and again, losing ourselves in its promise of a better place, where "dreams that you dare to dream really do come true." Forgetting where we were and why we were there, we sang more loudly than we should have, which brought my mother in again to hush us. We had always visited Grandma when she was sick and were always allowed to see her. Not this time.

My mother was on sick duty one day a week during Grandma's final illness; her sisters took turns the rest of the week. Grandma, who had raised eight children, chose to live alone after her husband died. All her children, two sons and five surviving daughters, contributed to her support and her care. Even the grandchildren had Grandma duties. We'd take turns walking to her flat on Garfield Place. I remember being sent to ask her if she needed anything, and then going to the grocery store for milk and butter and to the Italian bakery on her corner to buy what seemed a massive round of crusty bread. Understanding her instructions was sometimes a struggle. Though she'd lived more than fifty years in America, she had never learned to speak English. Yet she scolded me for not knowing Italian. "Shame on you," she would say.

In happier times, when she was well, the first thing Grandma would do when we arrived was offer us something to eat. But on the way to her house, my mother would tell us to say, "No, thank you" to whatever she offered. "Grandma doesn't have a lot of money, so don't eat her food." I declined when Grandma insisted we eat something because I was never hungry, but Eleanor, who always was, accepted the slice of bread and butter and glass of Ovaltine, and was smacked on the way home. "That's for not listening," my mother would say.

Grandma died a few weeks after Eleanor and I began our after-school vigils. No one knew how old she was; her birth records were in the old country. The date on her death certificate was an approximation. She was buried at St. John's, beside her husband. Her picture, in a matching oval frame, was added to the headstone. Looking back, I remember her as being old and ageless at the same time. She was a tall woman with a full figure; her hair was white and thick and coiled atop her head in a Gibson Girl bun. She wore no makeup; style was not a factor in her dress. She lived an unadorned life. It never mattered to any of us how old she was or how she looked. She was the glue that kept a large, multi-generational family together in difficult times.

It's been many decades since my grandmother died. Though she had always lived in the past, maintaining her Italian heritage while I had the promise of America ahead of me, she's an indelible part of my personal history. Even today, when I hear "Over the Rainbow," I am back in that dreary spare room with my sister, singing softly as Grandma lay dying. I like to think that our young voices, so full of hope for the future, eased her way over the rainbow as she passed from this life to the next.

Down Periscope!

The weekly swimming lessons at Manual Training High School in Brooklyn, New York were required more for safety than for fun at Coney Island. They served neither purpose for me. After two years of those dreaded hour-long sessions, I was still afraid of water deeper than I was tall, still afraid to put my head below the surface. In the end, all those lessons were a waste of taxpayers' money and my time. I could have been reading.

Mrs. Buckley, our swimming coach, ran along the side of the pool as I clung to its wall, afraid to let go as I neared the deep end, all the while blowing the whistle that hung around her neck and shouting, "Down periscope, Catherine!"

"Submerge, Catherine!"

"You'll never learn to swim if you don't get your head wet, Catherine!"

Which I always resented, because she never got anything wet. She never set foot, nor any other part of her ample body in the pool. She certainly didn't teach by example. I always wished I was brave enough to shout back, "I'll put my head in the water when you put yours in!" On the contrary, she took special precautions to keep her impeccably-coiffed, henna-treated hair dry at all times. Pity the hapless kid who jumped too vigorously into the pool and sent a splatter of chlorinated drops up to her helmet hair. Extra laps after class.

Fear of putting my head under water didn't start in Mrs. Buckley's class. When I was little, my mother used to wash my hair in the kitchen sink every Saturday morning. She dug her fingers into my scalp, working the shampoo into a voluminous lather. I wouldn't let her put my head under the faucet to rinse it away; she had to do it glass by glass.

Swimming was the only class I didn't mind failing, which I did every term, because its Pass or Fail grade did not figure into my scholastic average. I never had another swimming lesson after high school. Given the failure and humiliation I had suffered at the hands of Mrs. Buckley, I resolved that I would get through life without learning to swim.

Just as firmly, I resolved that my children would not. As soon as they were old enough for lessons, we joined a swimming club. At the beginning of summer I tipped the lifeguards generously and pointed out my son and daughter. "I can't swim," I told them. "I'm counting on you to keep an eye on them." Even with that precaution in place, I sat at the edge of the pool whenever one or both of them were in it, ready to sound the alarm if necessary.

Those days at the club were relaxing for the other mothers, a respite from their homemaking duties. They sat in circles of lounge chairs around the pool, enjoying coffee and conversation, trusting the lifeguards to watch over their kids. They were anxious times for me. Once during the morning session, and once again in the afternoon, the lifeguards blew their whistles and shouted, "All kids out of the pool! Now!" and Adult Swim began. The kids grudgingly pulled their waterlogged bodies out, their mothers jumped in, swam laps and dove off the board. Wearing my new Jantzen bathing suit, I bought one every year, I made my way to the shallow end of the pool, tugging at my flower-decorated swim cap to be sure it was secure; it didn't matter that it never got wet. I gingerly descended the four steps into the water and splashed around, waiting for the whistle that would send the kids back in.

Not being able to swim wasn't the only reason my self-esteem took a bashing at the pool. To maintain some semblance of order, the children's shoes were lined up neatly under their mothers' chairs. All around the pool, sneakers and sandals, two by two, revealed the size of the family and the fertility of the mother. My closest friend, who I always sat next to, had three pairs of sneakers for her boys and two pairs of sandals for her girls under her chair. Birthing a baby was an annual event for Anne. Whatever the age of your child, she had a playmate for it. One day, a woman came by, saw the one pair of sneakers and one pair of sandals beneath my chair and said sadly, as if offering condolences, "Oh, you have only two children."

41

When Amy and Bobby could swim the length of the pool and jump off the diving board, skills I thought would assure their safety in the water, I sent them to sleepaway camp. They spent their summers at Camp Chinqueka in Connecticut, where they learned to kayak and sail and water ski without fear. They grew up loving the water because they never had a frightening experience in it.

But neither did I. I wasn't tossed into deep water as a child and told to swim or sink, a barbaric test of youthful daring for some kids, imposed by their equally barbaric parents. I never walked in a lake when, without warning, the squishy bottom underfoot gave way and a precipitous drop sent me into panicky flailing and crying for help. I cannot say, "I almost drowned when I was young" when explaining my fear of the water. I was never in real danger at a pool, a beach or a lake because Eleanor always went in first and tested the waters for me. Because she was bold enough for both of us, I had a safety net that I hadn't earned.

Sundays were beach days at Coney Island for my family during the Depression. Picnics in the sand and a frolic in the ocean were affordable escapes from summer's oppressive heat. All four of my sisters and brothers learned to swim there. I had the same opportunities they had, and I should have learned long before I got to Mrs. Buckley's class. I used to think that if I'd had a better teacher then, I would be a swimmer now. But I have come to accept that my fear of the water is innate; I've stopped blaming Mrs. Buckley.

There is a paradox in my relationship with the water. Though I fear being in it, I love being near it. My happiest vacations have been at ocean beaches, the more tumultuous the crash of the waves pounding their shores, the more serene my state of mind. My final journey will be one I wasn't bold enough to take in life. I will set out to sea and float fearlessly in its infinite expanse.

The Substitute Bridesmaid

"**W**hen was this picture taken Nana? You look so pretty."

My teenage grandchildren were looking through an album of very old photos and saw a picture of a very young me. It was blurred and fuzzy, but there was no doubt I was dressed for a special occasion. It was taken the day I was a bridesmaid in my friend Annabelle's wedding. The photo is black and white, but I remembered the vibrant aqua of the chiffon skirt on the bridesmaid's dress I was wearing, the deeper blue of its lace bodice. A delicate wrap of chiffon draped around my shoulders made the dress modest enough for the church ceremony. My satin pumps were dyed to match the skirt. In my hair was a circle of miniature white flowers. I agreed with the kids. "I do look pretty, don't I?"

The photo brought me back many years and I lived again the ups and downs of a bittersweet friendship that I should have let go long before I did.

"I'm joining the sorority," Annabelle said, shifting nervously in her chair in our high school cafeteria, her eyes darting to the wall clock, listening for the bell that would send us back to class. In telling me that she had decided to join the sorority that had invited her, but not me, she was telling me she could no longer be my friend.

I told her it was okay, but it wasn't. For eight years there hadn't been an event in my life that didn't include Annabelle. We went through all the growing up stages together. We styled each other's hair; she taught me to dance, I helped her with her homework. She was accepted by my family as a part of who I was. When heads were counted for an occasion or an outing, hers was always one of them.

A shy child, I didn't have many friends. I didn't need them; I had Annabelle. My confidence in myself was rooted in the fact that she had chosen me to be her friend. Looking back at the black and white photos taken when we started Manual Training High School, now curled and brown-edged, I realize how naïve I was to think our friendship could overcome how differently we were developing. I had the look of a serious student; she had *sorority* written all over her. We would have started drifting apart anyway because we were beginning to set our goals in life and to reach them we would have to travel different paths. But I was thirteen when Annabelle abandoned me to join the sorority that had rejected me. I didn't understand that yet. I thought I would never fill the void she left in my life.

I did, of course. I joined academic clubs and met kids with goals like mine and teachers who helped us achieve them. We weren't part of the "in" crowd; we didn't party with the team after the football games. Our highs were being accepted into honor societies. My focus was on a much different future than the one Annabelle chose. I went on to college; she met and married Bill Green. I went to Manhattan to pursue a career in publishing; she filled her home with children, creating the big family she always wanted. We each found what we had needed most.

If this were a fairy tale, that would be the happy ending. But I left out a chapter. When Annabelle was planning her dream wedding, I was living my dream on Madison Avenue. We hadn't kept in touch. Then one day, she called. She had something to ask of me and was having a hard time getting it out.

"I don't know if I should ask you this," she said. "If you say no, I'll understand." A member of her bridal party, all of them sorority sisters, had dropped out. Would I take her place?

"Of course I will," I said.

And so she was married, surrounded by a full quota of bridesmaids, resplendent in a Cinderella ball gown with a hand-beaded bodice and layers of lace. She moved to New Jersey, a place people enter and, apparently, disappear. I heard about her occasionally, but I never heard from her. I moved on with my life, too. Wrapped up in my own career, marriage, children, and a move across the country, I forgot about Annabelle. She had moved out of my life once again.

Or so I thought. Decades later I found myself thinking about her, wondering how she was, where she was, *if* she was. I tried to find her on the internet, but a name like Green resulted in a million hits. I let it be known to mutual friends that I was searching for her. They didn't know where she was, either. Fifty years is a long time to be out of touch. But they wanted to help. I gave them the few statistics I had and they went to work. None of their searches led to a match.

I had just about given up hope of finding her when my daughter called. "I found Annabelle," she said. The woman she found was my age, born in Brooklyn, went to my high school and was now living in New Jersey. I had followed similar leads to a dead end, but I had a feeling this could be the one. There was no email address in my daughter's source, only a postal address. I wrote and mailed a letter, hoping it would mean something to the Annabelle who received it. I included my phone number, and closed with: "*If you are indeed my Annabelle, I would love to hear from you.*"

A week later, I found my husband standing by the phone when I came home. "There's a message for you," he said. "It's from Annabelle."

"My Annabelle?" I asked, frozen in place.

"Your Annabelle. She left a number. Call her back."

"I can't. I don't know what to say to her." It was then I realized that I never expected to receive a reply to my letter. Maybe I hadn't really wanted one. Maybe I should just let the past rest.

"Call her."

Our cross-country conversation lasted almost an hour. She told me she never went back to work after she married. I went back when my children were in school full time. She took me through the births and naming of all four of her babies, then went through the grandchildren, many of whom live just a visiting distance away. She had kept her family nest within easy reach. My two children live on opposite coasts; when I'm with one, I'm 3000 miles away from the other. She still lives in the house she moved into as a bride, and would never leave it, she said. When her husband's company was moving to another state, a non-commutable distance from their home, he left his job because she wouldn't leave her house. When our circumstances called for a major relocation that would take us away from our home of forty years, my husband and I weighed the pros and cons of the move on a yellow legal pad with a line drawn down its center. Once our decision was made, we moved on to what has become a new beginning for us.

Annabelle had found her niche in life and was happy in it. Her need to cling to the security of the known would not have worked for me. I've always needed to find out what else is out there. Our conversation helped me accept that our parting had been inevitable. Though I didn't think so at the time, our being set free to seek the life we each wanted was a good thing.

"I'm so glad I found you, Annabelle. Let's keep in touch."

The next month, at Christmas, I sent her a card. I didn't hear from her that Christmas, or ever again. I'm not disappointed. My search accomplished something I had subconsciously needed to do for a very long time: it closed an unfinished chapter in my life; it told me it was time to let go.

When my grandchildren found the picture of me dressed for Annabelle's wedding, I told them the story of the substitute bridesmaid. I was stunned by the force of their reactions.

"You *shouldn't* have!"

"*I* wouldn't have!"

"Why *did* you!"

They were unanimous in their outrage over Annabelle's request and their disbelief in my willingness to do it. Then I realized that their anger at Annabelle was based on their love for me. What they didn't understand is that my decision, all those years ago, was based on the love I still had for Annabelle.

Though I tell myself I have closed that chapter in my life, I admit that its fallout has endured. I make friends easily now, and I have many. But I have never again allowed myself to have a best friend.

More Than Sisters

It was 1948 and the world was once again a safe place for American students. The air raid drills whose sirens had brought lessons to an abrupt halt and sent us scrunching under our desks preparing for bombs that were never dropped, were a thing of the past. The final all-clear signal had sounded over intercom systems in schools across the nation, the era of peace and prosperity was beginning, and my high school years were coming to an end.

It was Senior Day at Manual Training High School in Brooklyn and I was a senior. I was eighteen and my sister Eleanor was twenty. She had graduated two years before and now worked as a secretary on Wall Street. She took the day off to be with me at this pre-graduation celebration.

To define us from the rest of the student body, and to collect our due in accolades, seniors were allowed to wear the academic gown we would graduate in. Excused from all classes, we strutted the halls, ignoring the bells that usually sent us scrambling to class, basking in the envy of lower grade students. We owned the day. In the afternoon, we presented the annual Senior Play to a general assembly in the auditorium. I had helped write it, and had a role in it. It was about the Pilgrims landing on Plymouth Rock. I played a Puritan woman, albeit one wearing lipstick and mascara. Throughout the day, we took group photos and wrote messages in each other's yearbooks pledging eternal friendship with kids who were two months away from dropping out of our lives.

The best part of the day for me was having Eleanor there. All my friends knew her because we were always together. We were a set; if you wanted one, you had to take the other, so much so that if I showed up alone, I was asked, "Where's Eleanor?"

Even at home, household chores were divided into two parts, one for each of us. Every morning, even on school days, Eleanor dusted the front half of our flat, I dusted the back half; every evening, Eleanor washed the dishes and I dried them. My mother never had a drainboard at her sink; she had no need for one. She always had two children of an age to wash and dry and dispatch the clean plates and glasses back to the cupboard, where they belonged. My mother didn't give us these chores because she was lazy; she felt it was her responsibility to train her daughters for woman's work. Eleanor and I didn't balk at the tasks because it was a time when children were expected to help out at home, but also because we were doing them together and we found ways to make them fun. We played word games and sang songs and forgot we were standing at a sink full of dirty dishes. Our father's last words to us as he left for work each day were, "Listen to your mother." It never occurred to us that we had an option.

Eleanor and I were almost clones in every way but looks. Our voices were very similar; one was often mistaken for the other on the phone. What amazes me even now is, though she was left-handed and I am right-handed, our handwriting was almost identical. Our physical traits, however, couldn't be more different. Eleanor's complexion was fair and sprinkled with freckles; mine was olive. Her hair was just the right shade of red, neither carrot-bright nor rusty-dull, said to have been inherited from our paternal grandmother but unverifiable because Grandma's hair was gray before she came to America. My mother rolled Eleanor's beautiful hair in rags every night. Unraveled in the morning, it fell in long, bouncy curls to her shoulder. My hair was dark brown and straight and cut to ear length by my godfather, who was a barber. He couldn't afford to buy me the presents other kids got from their godparents, so he came every Sunday and gave me a haircut instead. My mother said I had to accept them.

The facts of life as told to young children in those days were simple. In explaining our physical differences, my mother by-passed the stork and went straight to the cabbages. She had us believing that Eleanor came out of a red cabbage, and the cabbage I emerged from was black. If, as today's child psychologists claim, the first three years of life determine a child's future development, my future, defined by that black cabbage, should have been bleak.

Our bonding began early in life. Eleanor was in charge of my care whenever we were away from home. Just two years older than I am, she took on adult responsibilities and never considered them a burden. When I was well enough to go back to school after a bout of pneumonia the winter I was seven, it was Eleanor's responsibility to walk with me, making sure that my coat remained buttoned to my chin. She picked me up at three o'clock, buttoned me for the return trip, and delivered me safely to my mother. On my first day back, my mother dressed me with a sweater under my coat and sent me off with instructions not to take it off. When I got to class, I removed my coat and left the sweater on. Mrs. Dignan, my second-grade teacher, thought it wasn't healthy to be overdressed when the radiators were hissing out steamy warmth and told me to take it off.

"I can't," I said.

"Why not?" she asked.

"My mother said not to."

No amount of coaxing could get me to take my sweater off. She sent for my sister. When Eleanor arrived, Mrs. Dignan told her to tell me to take my sweater off.

"She can't" Eleanor said.

"Why not?"

"My mother said not to."

Mrs. Dignan conceded defeat and my sweater was no longer an issue. I kept it on in class until April when my father unwrapped his fig tree, in our family the acknowledged end of winter.

"Forget You Have A Mother!"

I had talked my mother into letting me go to college but that was only the first battle in what would be an ongoing war. The fight continued. I know now that the roadblocks my mother placed in my path were based on her fear that, by my growing in my world, she would diminish in hers. Independence for her youngest child threatened the nest that she had nurtured for so many years. I was about to add another dimension to her anxiety.

I was in my junior year at Hunter College in New York City when I saw a brochure on the bulletin board outside the Guidance Counselor's office that reawakened a dream I thought I had put to rest. It described a Summer Writers Conference at the University of Wisconsin-Madison.

The brochure spoke to all my aspirations. I have always been an avid reader, so of course I wanted to be a writer; in my mind, it was a natural progression. That's why I was at Hunter. It was the only school in the City University of New York system that offered a degree in Journalism. Brooklyn College, also a CUNY school, was within walking distance of home, but I opted for an hours-long subway ride to get the degree I wanted. I was within a year of achieving my goal when I happened upon the brochure that sent me back into battle with my mother.

I rode the subway home that night with visions of the Madison campus dancing in my head. The photo on the cover of the brochure showed a quintessential university quad, its lush lawns the heartbeat of campus life. Even on paper, the students gathered on its lawns wearing Badger sweatshirts they would outgrow but never throw out, seemed to be defining their lives, creating a personal history. A stately bell tower, the classic symbol of academia, was the centerpiece of this landscape. I wanted to be there so badly, I could hear its chimes pealing the school anthem.

But here I was at Hunter College, its halls of learning inside a complex of tall stone buildings devoid of architectural history or elegance, a stark contrast to the university pictured in the brochure. It was, in my time, an urban campus with direct access to the subway many of its students rode to its doors. My daily schedule was an hour and a half subway ride from Brooklyn to East 68th Street in Manhattan, a full day of classes, a bus ride down to my part-time job at Macy's on 34th Street, followed by the subway ride home and hours of required reading before I fell into bed and set the alarm for an early rise.

I had been living this routine for three years when I saw the brochure describing a very different student life. Its promise fell on fertile ears.

The next day, I took that dank underground ride to school resolved to hang-in for the remaining year of study that would complete my degree requirements. During my lunch break, I found myself walking by the Guidance Counselor's office again. I stood before the bulletin board, breathless with longing to be on that quad. I looked around; there was no one in the hall but me. I touched the brochure, and knew I couldn't leave without it. I removed the tack, tucked the brochure in a notebook, and made my getaway. I didn't look at it again until I got home. I waited until after dinner and after I had done all my homework, keeping it for last, like a child who has to eat every pea on his plate before he can have dessert. It was past midnight, the rest of the family was asleep. I settled onto the couch with the brochure and wallowed in my impossible dream. I could see myself on that quad, like June Allyson in the movie "Best Foot Forward." I could hear myself singing "Buckle down Wisconsin, buckle down, you can win Wisconsin if you buckle down." (The college doing the buckling down in the movie was the fictional Winsocki.)

The tuition for the conference and transportation to Wisconsin would cost $500. Where would I get that kind of money? I was barely making enough at Macy's to pay for my books. Then I remembered the insurance policy. During the Depression, many mothers took out insurance policies on family members. It was their security blanket during a notoriously insecure time. Somehow, they found the ten cents per policy to hand over to the insurance agent who came to collect it each week. They had different reasons for buying the policies. For some it was for a sudden illness or, God forbid, a funeral. My mother's policies for her three girls were for a specific purpose: They would pay for our weddings. They afforded her a great measure of satisfaction; she would do right by her girls when the time came. She had already cashed in both my sisters' policies for their weddings. Mine would be ready for me when I was ready for it. But I wasn't a young girl dreaming of a beautiful wedding. I didn't have fantasies where I saw myself floating down the center aisle of St. Francis Xavier Church, veiled in white, clinging to my father's arm, my love waiting for me at the end of my triumphal march. I never had that dream. I was putting nothing at risk by using my wedding money for another purpose.

I knew my mother would be appalled by my plan for her insurance money, but I was so intent on my urgent need for it now, that I didn't appreciate her need to keep it for its original purpose, no matter how far-off. It wouldn't be easy to get her to release her hold on that policy. I knew, too, that it wasn't just the money I would have to fight for. I would also have to overcome her ingrained belief that girls did not leave home alone for any reason, not overnight, and certainly not for a summer. In fact, this would be the more difficult battle. My mother started with that when I showed her the brochure.

"You're not thinking of going there, are you?" she asked, incredulously. "You know you can't go away by yourself." We had many "discussions," usually over dinner. My father sat at the head of the table, but I knew it was my mother I would have to persuade. Throughout my childhood, if I asked something of my father, he would say, "Sure Honey, if it's okay with your mother." In Italian immigrant families, Honor Thy Mother was part of our DNA.

I had just about convinced her that I was no longer a child and could take care of myself, when she asked, "How are you going to pay for this?" I took a deep breath, and plunged in.

"I'd like to use my wedding money now." She gave me a look that said, *Whose child is this?*

"Do you know how many years it took to save that money, how I sacrificed to scrape those dimes together?" I cringed, but I rose to the challenge. I was already in deep water; it was swim or sink now. "I'm not going to get married for a long time," I told her, which was the wrong way to start my plea. She was eager for me to be "settled," which for an Italian mother was to see her daughters married and safely in someone else's care. "I want to finish school," I continued, "and get a job in New York, and travel, all those things. I may never get married." I added quickly, "But if I do, I'll pay for the wedding myself, I promise." My mother sat there in shock. One more daughter to see settled and her work would be done. And here was her youngest, always the most obedient, stepping out of the cocoon of safety she was raised in, shattering her peace of mind.

Finally, beaten down by the unrelenting pressure I applied day and night, and also because she was older now and some of the fight had gone out of her, she acquiesced, but not before making a last-stand effort to put an end to my rebellion: "Okay, you can go," she said sternly, arms folded across her chest in the defy-me-if-you-dare position I grew up with, "but forget you have a mother!" Ecstatic, I ran to the phone, dialed a classmate who was going to Madison, and shouted, "My mother said I can go!" Later, I learned from Eleanor that my mother was devastated at how readily I had discarded her, "Without a moment's hesitation." I never believed for a minute that she meant her threat, and I was right. I was away eight weeks and a food package was delivered to my dorm every week. I was the most popular girl on the floor, thanks to the mother who had disowned me. Years later, I kept that promise I made her. When I married, I paid for the wedding.

Three courses were offered in the University of Wisconsin Writers Conference that summer. I registered for all three, and failed all three. I wasn't there to learn to write, but rather to learn to live, on my own, without my usual support systems, and without retreating into what had always been my refuge, a book. My sister Rose, eleven years older than I am, got through the Depression and World War II without seeking solace in books and scoffed at my need for them. "All that book learning and no common sense," is how she described me. It was time to see if she was right.

I was also there to experience the flip side of college life as I knew it. After classes, I spent lazy summer afternoons on the quad, even more beautiful in life than in the brochure. I met friends in the student Rathskeller and learned to play bridge. I never opened the volume of George Bernard Shaw, required reading for the playwriting course. I went to the library not to study, but to luxuriate in its comfort. I lounged in the upholstered chairs set in study clusters by windows looking out on the quad. If I read at all, it was something by a Brontë, any Brontë, I loved them all. It was a guilty pleasure, reading just for the joy of it. Not having to get to a job after class, I took part in extra-curricular activities as I never had at Hunter. I campaigned for a roommate running for Dorm Queen riding through campus in an open convertible, wearing paper rabbit ears and shouting into a megaphone, "Vote for Bunny Banks!" That's as close as I came to June Allyson. I wasted none of this precious time away from those austere stone towers back East on academic pursuits. I was failing my classes and I didn't care because I was passing another test: I went from timid to not-so-timid. It was a beginning.

When I look back at my college years, Hunter is a blur. But that summer on that campus in Madison is as fresh in my mind now as it was then. My Badger sweatshirt has traveled with me from home life to married life, and has even made the trip across the country to my new life.

I grew up in a culture where I had to fight for things that were considered a man's birthright. Most of my battles were with my mother. She didn't understand that the world I would live in one day would be much different from the world she had lived her life in. She was preparing me to live in a world that I knew was on the way out.

Ironically, my mother is the one who taught me to fight, not knowing that one day we would be on opposite sides of the same battles, and I would win them by using the strength I got from her, against her. In spite of my mother's explosive order to forget her, there isn't a day in my life that I don't remember her. Though she never wanted for me the things I wanted for myself, I think she would understand now why I needed them.

Radio Voices

B eing a girl in a family with three men, all of whom were rabid Brooklyn Dodgers fans, my summers were defined by baseball even though I had no interest in the game. Red Barber, the Dodgers sportscaster, was an ever-present voice in our house, as beloved as "Dem Bums" themselves. On weekends, two radios blasted two different games, one tuned into the Dodgers, the other to the Yankees. If you were a Dodgers fan, you automatically hated the Yankees because they were winners and their fans never let you forget it. The Dodgers won their games with the blood, sweat and prayers of their fans; the Yankees racked up their wins with the help of Babe Ruth and Joe DiMaggio.

My brothers ran the length of our railroad flat, from the dining room in the back to the living room in the front, cheering a Dodgers hit, cheering even louder for a Yankees strikeout. I didn't care who won or lost, but there was no escaping the broadcasts on those stifling days of summer when windows and doors were thrown open in search of a breeze. The whole neighborhood was tuned in to the game. Wherever I was—in the house, the backyard, on the stoop—Red Barber's voice was there, too.

There was another baseball radio voice, that of Mel Allen, who called the play-by-play for the Yankees games in a tone that was just as smug as the team he spoke for. Hardly objective, his exuberant "How about that!" after every Yankees gain left no doubt as to whose side he was on and added to the bad blood between teams and fans. This wasn't just a game, it was weekend warfare.

My brothers weren't just baseball fans, they played the game, too. On Friday afternoons I went with my father to the Park Circle athletic field to root for Lou, who played third base on the Hilfords, our neighborhood team, and Joe, who was in the outfield. I didn't want to go, and once there, I didn't want to stay. It was hot and dusty; the clouds of dirt sent up by runners sliding into base, made my throat dry and itchy. "I'm thirsty," I'd whine. As often as necessary, my father summoned the soda vendor, who wore a cooler strapped around his shoulders, to get me through to the ninth inning. He never left a game before it ended.

Trips to the beach, or Sunday visits with family were timed not to conflict with a game. If there was a tie at the end of the ninth and the game went into extra innings, social plans across the board were adjusted. This was understood and accepted by all. It was also a factor on the day I graduated from college.

My mother ordered me to leave for the ceremony much earlier than I had to. I didn't understand why, but she said "Go!" and I went. Hours later, degree in hand, I was greeted with shouts of "Surprise!" when I came home. An army of aunts had swarmed in after I left and set up a party in my honor, the same aunts who never understood why my mother had let me go to college in the first place. My mother, who had also been a con in the debate about higher education for me, was the first one ready to leave for the graduation exercises. She had made command attendance calls to all my siblings, who dared not make other plans.

Only one person was missing as the time drew near to leave for Hunter College. Mom paced anxiously, muttering to herself, "Where is that man? He said he'd be back by now." The missing person was my father.

Dad worked for himself and was free to do things other fathers couldn't. Sometimes, on a hot summer afternoon, he'd come home and rescue my mother from the kitchen. We'd put on bathing suits and head for Coney Island for a cooling dip in the Atlantic and dinner at Nathan's Famous hotdog stand. Whenever he could get away, he went to a weekday Dodgers game, which is where he was on my graduation day—at Ebbets Field. There was an afternoon game between the Brooklyn Dodgers and the Chicago Cubs and it went into extra innings. I've always considered the fact that my father left the ballpark before the game ended one of the greatest expressions of his love for me. And his fear of my mother.

The Dodgers won that game with the Cubs when Carl Furillo hit a homer with two men on in the bottom of the 10th. They say the earth shook around Ebbets Field from the roar of the crowd and their lusty rendition of the team's rowdy theme song, "Follow the Dodgers." My father missed it all. He was watching his daughter march into the Hunter College auditorium to the soul-stirring strains of "Pomp and Circumstance."

To Be Or Not To Be

When I was very young, my cousin Filly (a nickname for the hated Filomena) told me I had ruined my mother's perfect family. A perfect family, Filly explained, was one with two boys and two girls, just like her mother's, and like my mother's was before I was born. And it couldn't be fixed, she declared. "She can't send you back." With that, she skated off, leaving me in tears.

Many years later, Eleanor and I were having a glass of wine and growing nostalgic about our childhood in that Brooklyn brownstone where the doors were always open, the tables were always set, a mother was always there to receive a child. We remembered stories we thought were long forgotten.

"Remember when Filly told me I ruined Mom's perfect family?" I asked.

"Well, Filly couldn't be more wrong," Eleanor replied. "I can't imagine my life without you. I'm so glad Mom flushed that medicine down the toilet."

"What?"

"Oh," she said, hesitantly. "I forgot—you don't know."

"I don't know what?"

"I guess it's okay to tell you now. Mom didn't do it, after all, here you are," she said, trying to make light of her slip. I could sense that she was uneasy, she didn't want to continue this conversation. With a shaky hand, she re-filled her glass. "I'll be right back," she said, jumping up suddenly, sending drops of wine splashing across the table. I knew she was going for her cigarettes; they were the lifeline that saw her through many a crisis. She returned clutching a pack of Marlboros in one hand and an ashtray in the other, a familiar scene. Even when we talked on the phone and she said, "Hold on a minute," I knew she was going in search of cigarettes and an ashtray. Lighting one now, she inhaled deeply and exhaled carefully, away from my face.

"Start at the beginning," I said, motioning her away when she offered to refill my glass. I leaned in as Eleanor began to unfold a story she had held close for many years.

Towards the end of her life, my mother lived with Eleanor at her seaside home in Belle Harbor, New York, a community kind to those at both ends of life's range. Eleanor was a patient listener; she loved to hear Mom talk about old times. One summer afternoon, they sat on the porch waving to the steady stream of young families passing by on their way to the beach.

Eleanor broke open a new pack of cigarettes, her second of the day; Mom snapped dying yellow leaves off the potted geraniums. The conversation, as always, went back in time. This day, my mother told Eleanor about the dilemma she had faced before I was born, and the decision she'd had to make.

It was 1930, one year after the Wall Street stock market crashed, ushering in the worst economic depression the country had ever faced. My father's soft-drink business was floundering. "When they learned Mom was pregnant again," Eleanor said, "they didn't think they could support another child."

She paused, waiting for a reaction from me. I said nothing. "They might have thought about it for me, too," she said, rushing in to fill the silence. "But here we both are," she finished, with an attempt at a laugh that didn't quite make it.

"Go on," I said.

Sighing, she began to re-live the pain of that long-ago conversation. "Mom was so distressed over the pregnancy that when Dad said he'd ask Bruno if he had something to end it, she agreed." Bruno was the neighborhood pharmacist who families took their medical problems to because they couldn't afford to see a doctor. He always shook up something in a bottle that made them feel better. The colors varied. My mother's nerve medicine, a brilliant red, never failed to calm her anxieties. My ongoing sore throat was treated with a teaspoon of a bright yellow blend that soon had me swallowing without pain.

"When Dad brought home the bottle of Bruno's medicine," Eleanor continued, "He told Mom whether she decided to take it, or not, would be all right with him."

My heart ached for my mother at this point in the story. Tears burned against my eyelids. I couldn't think of a more difficult decision to be confronted with. But my mother was a woman who didn't flinch when it came to making tough decisions. She poured Bruno's medicine into the toilet and flushed it down.

I can't help wondering what led to her decision. Was it because she was a devout Catholic and she feared she would be punished in the next life for making a mortal sin in this one? Did she fear the medicine might damage her general health? Might it even take her life, leaving her four young children without a mother?

Eleanor had mixed feelings about telling me this story. "I'm relieved that I no longer have to live with the secret," she said. "But I hope I haven't hurt you in telling it." I assured her that she hadn't. The tears I had not allowed to flow would have been for my mother, not for me.

My tenuous beginnings may subconsciously be the reason I've been a lifelong Pollyanna. Maybe, having survived at all, I am at peace with what is, not dwelling on the uncertainties of what if. I didn't inherit that trait from my mother. Her sky was always falling, but she was fierce in her determination to keep it from falling on me. I wonder now, were her extraordinary efforts to keep me safe, to keep me well, to keep me near, a reflection on my shaky start in life? She was a diligent mother to all her children, but I was raised in a more encompassing safety net than my siblings. I always thought it was because I was the youngest, but after Eleanor's revelation, I believe there was more to it than that. I think my mother never forgot how strongly she had been tested and how close she had come to making a decision she would always regret.

After Eleanor died, I told my daughter the story of my ambivalent start in life. She understood the circumstances that had prompted my parents to consider ending the pregnancy. What she had a hard time accepting is why my sister had revealed that long-kept secret. "You didn't have to know that," she said. But I did. At last, I understood why my mother didn't just hold my hand, she gripped it. It was many years before I could loosen her grasp, many struggles before I could break away and, finally, move away. She never got over the shock of either. Now I knew why.

Little Mary

We had a secret in my family when I was growing up. Her name was "Little Mary."

Little Mary was born before I was, to an aunt I never knew. Her mother, my Aunt Mary, died in childbirth. This aunt's life was, and still is, a mystery to me. The few photos I've seen of her tell me she was the prettiest of my mother's sisters, but more reserved. She appeared to be neither as flamboyant as Aunt Anna, nor as feisty as Aunt Grace, and certainly not as formidable as Aunt Susie, whose edicts neither child nor adult dared defy. When Aunt Mary was spoken of, it was in whispers, cloaked in sadness. When we kids asked, "Where's Little Mary's mother?" the only response was, "Be kind to your cousin." We shared our beds, we shared our toys, but no one shared our cousin's history with us.

Motherless, Little Mary was cared for by my mother and her sisters the first two years of her life. The infant was passed from one aunt to another, each trying to give her the love she would never know from her mother. When her father, Uncle Frank, remarried, it was to a woman who wanted him but not his child. She was forced to raise Little Mary, but couldn't find it in her heart to love her. She abused her, both physically and emotionally. When the abuse was severe, Uncle Frank brought his daughter to her aunts to heal. Physically, there were bruises and scars; once she arrived with evidence of a cigarette burn on her arm. But the hurt in her eyes, her guarded manner, told an even sadder story. When she arrived for a stay, she was wary at first. It was a while before she believed she was out of harm's way.

The aunts were outraged each time Uncle Frank arrived at their door with his battered child. They demanded that he leave his wife, or leave the child with them. He refused to do either.

Little Mary, a powerless pawn, spent her early years shuttling between the stepmother who broke her and the aunts who put her back together.

We never knew when she would leave us. When Uncle Frank reappeared, unannounced, we knew our cousin's visit was over. Her clothes were hurriedly packed, the children were gathered to hug her goodbye, and none of us knew when, or if, we would see her again. In time, the separation did become permanent. When she was four years old, Uncle Frank moved his family South and Little Mary moved out of our lives. The aunts never heard from her again, nor did she contact any of her cousins when she grew up. Our memories of her faded.

This happened when I was too young to understand anything except that my cousin was visiting for a while. Now, decades after she left us, I am haunted by questions I wish I had asked earlier. My mother, who was close to all her sisters all her life, never talked about the sister she had lost. There were no stories of their childhood together. It was almost as if this sister had never been a part of her life. It wasn't because that's how death was dealt with in those days. My grandfather died long before I was born, yet my grandmother kept his memory alive for all of us. Except for the care they gave her daughter, I have no memory of my mother, her sisters, or my grandmother talking about Aunt Mary.

Thinking about this so many years later, I am consumed with sadness for my cousin, who made sudden appearances in my life and just as suddenly vanished. All these years later, I still have a vivid picture of what she looked like in my mind. She was fair-skinned with straight, chin-length black hair; bangs rested on her brows just above her sad brown eyes.

As a memoirist, I feel incomplete never having known my Aunt Mary, nor anything about her. All my mother's sisters and their children were vivid characters in my childhood. Writing about them reminds me of the two vacancies in my memory bank: The aunt whose unique traits should have been stored there, too, waiting for me to call them up when I started looking back, and the cousin who is a blank in my family history.

Her aunts knew nothing of the life Little Mary went on to after she left their care. They died not knowing what happened to her. At reunions of the cousins, we remember her only in sadness, and wonder why she has never tried to reconnect with us. Uncle Frank, eager to sever relations with his dead wife's family, never sent his new address, so we couldn't contact her. The cousins are scattered all over the country now; maybe she's tried and can't reach us, either. Or maybe she has chosen not to remember her traumatic beginnings. Maybe by not looking back, she was free to move forward.

She Came With Instructions

Unlike infants born to first-time mothers, my first child came with written instructions. When Mrs. Wolfe, our case-worker at the adoption agency, placed a sweet-smelling, five pound two ounce baby girl in my arms, she handed Phil an envelope containing two typewritten pages titled, "How Your Baby Likes to Spend Her Day."

The explicit details on those pages defined how I would spend my day, too: It would revolve entirely around my baby's schedule, tending to her when she was awake, and preparing for her next awake session while she slept. The day started early for both of us.

5:00 a.m.

Your baby wakes up at this time and wants to be changed and fed. She is cheerful, and likes to play for a while after her bottle.

It's now 6 a.m. I am not ready for play.

8:30 a.m.

Your baby will wake from a short nap and likes to have her bath and get ready for the day. She prefers her bath water at a medium temperature. She will take her vitamins now, from the dropper.

Wet babies are slippery, I learn. All the while she is in the water, I fear she will go under the water. I grasp her arm as fiercely as my mother grasped my hand as we stood at the edge of the ocean.

9 a.m.

It is now time for your baby's second bottle. She will like to go outside afterwards.

Where does an infant like to go at 9 a.m. on a blustery winter day in New York? My mother was a great believer in the health benefits of being outdoors. Each of her babies received the Required Daily Minimum of fresh air time. I hope she's not watching.

1:00 p.m.

Your baby will wake from her morning nap and be hungry for her third bottle. When she has finished, she will enjoy playing for a while.

My mid-day break. Nothing required of me except listening to the sounds of a baby enchanted with her own foot. I watch from the couch as a tiny foot appears above the rim of the bassinet. Minutes later, a tiny hand reaches up and grabs that foot. Joyous gurgling erupts.

5:00 p.m.

At this time, your baby will look forward to her fourth bottle. She likes to watch television and be cuddled after this. Then, she will be ready to be dressed for bed.

I begin to think about dinner for her father.
Remember him?

9:00 p.m.

Your baby takes her last bottle at this time and should sleep all night. However, your baby may wake up at 1:00 a.m. once in a while. She will like to be changed, and may want some milk or water.

Once in a while? Neither baby nor mother sleeps through the night for many months. Our chair rocks soundlessly through the hushed hours before dawn, our breathing synchronized, our need for each other met.

Amy was born after Christmas, and came to live with us before Easter. That Christmas, Phil and I gave each other a baby shower. The gifts under the tree were wrapped in the red and green of the holiday season, but everything inside was pink. We shopped separately and didn't tell each other what we bought. They were the most exciting gifts we had ever exchanged. One of them, a miniature pink felt stocking with green rick-rack edging and brightly-colored sequins sprinkled over all, was immediately placed on the tree, front and center. It has occupied the same spot every Christmas since, hung by Amy herself as soon as she was able. It now hangs on her tree, in her home, an aging symbol of a love that never grows old.

Knowing When To Quit

I like to think I've lived my life as someone who doesn't give up. Hang in there. Follow your dream. You can do it. Platitudes all, but I have tried to push myself forward against all odds. Or, as Leah thinks, "...always kept my hand up." But knowing when to quit has served me just as well.

I had been working as secretary to the creative director at the Raymond Spector Advertising Agency on Madison Avenue in Manhattan. We had just one account that was so lucrative, we didn't need any others. That account was Hazel Bishop Lipstick, which we promised in all our ads, was "Kiss-proof— It stays on you, not on him."

Women fell for the lie and bought the lipstick. The slogan and the campaign were so successful that we ran modified versions of the ad with the same slogan for the three years I worked there. My boss, the creative director who wasn't allowed to be creative, drowned his frustrations in long, liquid lunches. I, too, could have written those ads in my sleep, so I began covering for him by meeting the deadlines he missed.

When this had gone on for a while, I asked him if I could move up to a copywriting job. He agreed to speak to Mr. Spector on my behalf. He reported back to me, using Mr. Spector's exact words: "Why take a good secretary and make her a bad copywriter?" Request denied. I went home seething that night. The next morning, I marched into Mr. Spector's office without knocking, and announced, "I quit."

Determined not to take another secretarial job, I spent a month creating a portfolio of bogus ads that had never run. I didn't think they would fool the people who interviewed me, but at least they showed I could write. I started answering want ads at agencies, magazines and book publishers. After canvassing several ad agencies without success, I answered an ad for a copywriter at Parents' magazine. Its offices were located at 52 Vanderbilt Avenue, and I didn't know how to get there. My father, who always helped me with directions, didn't know either. "When you get to Grand Central Station," he said, "find the taxi stand and take one to Vanderbilt Avenue."

Dressed in my navy blue interview suit and pristine white gloves, I got into a cab and, in my most worldly voice, I announced my destination; "52 Vanderbilt Avenue, please."

The driver turned to face me. "That would be across the street," he said. "Think you can walk that far?"

My composure was shattered, but I got the job.

I worked in Manhattan for ten years after that. The barbs of surly cab drivers didn't change, but I did. I walked the city, getting lost and finding my way with the help of strangers. I spent weekends exploring the many delights of Central Park. My jobs were mostly on the East Side, but I crossed over to the West Side to experience the thrills of Broadway. I accelerated my pace, became attuned to the rhythms of the city, and made it my own.

I didn't do it alone. The woman who hired me at Parents' started out as my boss then became my mentor and a lifelong friend. She took me under her wing and I followed her lead, not only on the job, but after hours, too, as she introduced me to her city and the world beyond. She passed her passion for Paris on to me, unveiling the delights of a fabled city to a young girl who's been infatuated with it ever since. How different my life would have been had I not walked away from the Raymond Spector Advertising Agency in a snit.

Big Blue

I became an IBMer by accident. I had never wanted to work in a corporate environment, with their set-in-stone rules and regulations, where employees conform to a company identity and individual creativity is stifled. In the 1950's, IBM was the dominant giant looming over corporate America. In my mind, we had no future together.

I was in my late fifties and between jobs when I decided to try temping for a while. One temporary agency rejected me because of my age, but another received me with open arms when they learned I could write; age was not an issue. Their client, the IBM Watson Research Center, three miles from my home, was looking for someone with writing skills to sit in a week-long meeting of scientists brainstorming a new concept, take notes, and write a report of their conclusions. I would do this on a computer. This was a time when anyone over 50 suffered from acute computer phobia. We were, literally, afraid of the damn things. I flinched when the recruiter mentioned IBM and confessed that I had never sat at a computer. "I'll pass on this one," I said. "What else do you have?" But she insisted. "They're not asking for someone with computer experience, they'll teach you the few skills you'll need. Go for the interview. The job is just for three weeks. You might learn something."

I went for the interview and got the job. That three-week temporary assignment took six weeks to complete. By that time, I had overcome my fear of computers and I accepted the offer to join the company as a recruiter of college students to fill our internship program. Nothing has had a greater influence on both my professional and personal lives than being pushed, against my will, into the technology age.

I owe another debt to IBM. Finally, in retirement, I was able to satisfy my lifelong yearning to study at renowned universities. My summer at the University of Wisconsin as an undergraduate had opened the door and I was now free and had the means to walk through it again. Big Blue softened the blow of its first major employee layoffs in the economic downturn of the 1990's with generous pensions and perks, one of which was a stipend to spend on education and other pursuits that would enhance retired life. I spent mine on summer writing workshops at Cornell University and Vassar college. I chose Cornell because it had been my son's school and I remembered being overwhelmed with nostalgia as I stood on its beautiful quad the first time I visited him. Tears rolled down my cheeks as the bell tower pealed the school anthem and I was back in Madison, thirty years younger, believing the future could be anything I wanted it to be.

With IBM's help, I went back long after Bob graduated and I met a woman who had received her law degree at Cornell the year I was born. For once, I wasn't the oldest student in the class. She was feisty and friendly and we hung out together. Her stories about her ground-breaking achievements in a man's educational setting were inspiring. I was awed to learn that gender and age were never issues with her, neither in college nor at the New York law firm where she rose to partner. I was invited to a party in her honor at the Yale Club in New York, located at 50 Vanderbilt Avenue. This time I knew how to get there.

The corporate world that for many years I had thought of as stifling opened broad new vistas for me. My time there enlightened my perception of other countries, other people. In my job as a recruiter of summer interns, I canvassed the northeastern universities in search of the best and the brightest students, many of them here on visas from India, China, Pakistan, Japan. The halls of the Research Center rang with many languages. We came together in classes and clubs and learned more than job-related matters from each other. I had never worked in an employee environment so varied in cultures, yet so alike in goals and corporate identity—which, I had to concede, was not a bad thing, after all.

Who's Listening?

Public speaking is high on the list of things people fear. That's not true of me. I am often asked to speak at testimonials and family occasions. I spoke at Leah's Bat Mitzvah when she turned thirteen. My speech was so well-received that one of the guests, a woman I had never met before, asked me to speak at her son's Bar Mitzvah the following month.

But even the success of that talk is dwarfed by the response to the many eulogies I've delivered. I get fan mail on those. People still breathing want to book me in advance for when they no longer are.

It all started when I took that temporary job at IBM. I signed on for three weeks and stayed for five years. The exalted leader of the technology pack at the time, Big Blue was flush with success and cash and spent extravagantly on enrichment programs for its employees. I studied the list of courses offered and narrowed it down to two possibilities, Ballroom Dancing or the Toastmasters Club. I chose public speaking over dancing knowing it would be a challenge, but not as great as staying in frame as I glide across a dance floor. I took the plunge and signed up to deliver the ten speeches required to earn my Competent Communicator Certificate.

Looking back on my life, I can't say I've always made the right decision when presented with a choice. Public speaking was never one of my goals, but the decision to learn to speak, rather than dance, was one of my best. Having survived childhood as the introvert in a family of extroverts vying for attention, I know now that by learning to speak in public, I was making up for not being heard at home. When family decisions, big and small, were being made, I didn't get a vote. I didn't care at the time. Let one of the others choose the movie we would see on Friday night and decide whether we would share Goobers or Milk Duds. Let someone else decide whether we would vacation at the beach or in the mountains the coming summer. I was more concerned with which books I would take out of the library the next week.

I was a painfully shy child and more than willing to have others speak for me. As a young adult, going out into the world, I had overcome my shyness and learned to speak for myself. Still, no one at home was listening. I thought marriage and motherhood would come with an automatic upgrade; they did not. When we gathered around dining room tables on holidays, there were lively discussions on everything from family matters to politics. I used to think my siblings hadn't heard my contributions to the conversations, but I know now they weren't listening.

It was a revelation to me when I learned, late in life, that my sisters and brothers weren't listening to each other, either. My six-year-old grandson sat halfway up the staircase adjacent to the dining room one Thanksgiving, puzzled by the boisterous scene at the table below. Later, he asked, "Nana, if everybody's talking at once, who's listening?" It took a child to reveal to me what I had missed all those years: The world-class speakers I grew up with didn't care if no one was listening.

But I did, so I learned to speak in places where I know I will be heard. What surprises me now about my public speaking is how much this once shy kid enjoys having the spotlight on her. When my name is announced and I begin the walk to the stage, my apprehension becomes excitement. I take my place behind the podium and carefully arrange my script atop it. I adjust the mic. I wait for the audience to hush, and when all eyes are on me, I speak—and *they* listen.

Out-Of-Sync

All my adult life I've been out-of-sync with the women of my generation. Though we were the same age, they were always years ahead of me in reaching life's milestones. More significantly, I was always years behind them. They married long before I did, started families when I was starting a career, enjoyed the rewards of grandparenting while I was still in the throes of raising teenagers. They segued gently into retirement, cutting their engines when I was revving up mine. Being the youngest child in a large family, it took me longer to grow up, to do the things a woman does, in the right order, at the right time. I was a late-bloomer.

When I married and moved to the suburbs, that hotbed of frantic mothering, the women who had children my children's age were tennis-playing Barbie dolls with whom I had nothing in common but our kids. My pre-school son had no one his age to play with in our neighborhood. He became a moving-van chaser, investigating every new family as it moved in, hoping to find a boy who would be his friend. One day he came running home, excited. "Mom, there's a boy my age in the new family!" Needing a friend myself, I asked, "What's the mother like?"

"She's a teenager," he said.

My son and that boy became best friends and that "teenage" mother and I are still friends. This was one case where age wasn't a factor for either of us. However, at a Christmas party she gave, I was introduced to another mother of a four-year-old boy. "You're Bobby's mother?" she asked. "I can't believe we have a child the same age." I felt more like Methuslah's mother than Bobby's.

I volunteered for every school activity. I was always the oldest mother on the bus that took the class to the Bronx Zoo or the Museum of Natural History. I baked carloads of cupcakes for fund-raising sales to pay for more bus rides to places that I didn't want to go. Though city-bred and not attuned to the wonders of nature, I went camping with Amy's Brownie troop to prove I could do anything the young mothers could. I couldn't. I answered all future calls to sleep in a tent with, "Just tell me how many cupcakes you need."

When at last both my kids were out of kindergarten and in school all day, I reentered the workplace. I needed to return to a world that was a better fit for me. It had been ten years since my last job; I was ready to rejoin my peers in a profession I loved. Alas, the publishing world I returned to was awash in young interns just out of college. Once again, I was out-of-sync.

My boss and mentor at Parents' magazine, gave me sound advice on aging which, for the most part, I've followed. "A woman should never tell her age," she said. "It puts her in a box." When she first passed that mantra on to me, I didn't understand it. As I aged, it became quite clear: The world defines a woman by her age, socially as I was defined at that Christmas party, and more important, professionally, which can result in denied opportunities. I was between publishing jobs and not yet ready to seek another permanent position when I registered with a temporary agency that placed office clerical workers. I thought being a receptionist for a few months would be just what I needed before plunging into another demanding job. I prepared a resume listing my earlier clerical jobs and, dressed carefully in my Ralph Lauren blazer over a crisp white shirt, I presented my best professional self to the receptionist at the agency. I was interviewed by a recruiter who assured me they would have no trouble placing me. She kept my resume and my ID to pass on to a second recruiter, then asked me to sit outside until that recruiter was free to interview me.

While I sat in the waiting room, a young gum-chewing woman, sloppily dressed, hair flying, came in and went directly to the office of the recruiter I had just seen where she was loudly called down for not showing up for an assignment the previous day. She was sent out on another job immediately. *This is going to be easy,* I thought. Then I heard the second recruiter call into the first, office to office, "Didn't you notice—she's 58?" My interviewer came out to the waiting room and returned my driver's license ID. "We have nothing for you today," she said. "We'll keep your resume on file." I never heard from them. From that day on, I told my age to no one but my doctors.

Challenges

In my family, none of the women drove. My mother and my sisters, all those aunts and cousins—not one of them could drive, or ever wanted to. They had husbands and brothers and grown sons who delivered them where they wanted to go and picked them up when they were ready to come home. There were also train stations and bus stops within easy reach. That's how I had navigated city life, too. But if I was to survive in the suburb I moved to when I was married, I would have to learn to drive. Once my husband boarded the 8:12 commuter train to his job in Manhattan, there was no way for me to get to the children's schools and supermarkets, vital destinations in a young mother's life.

Early Sunday mornings, Phil took me to the grounds of the Catholic convent in our town where there was a parking area large enough for me to practice turns and signals and parallel parking. Another plus was the lack of pedestrians, except for the nuns in residence. When we arrived, they would be strolling in pairs in spiritual communion with their Lord, strands of prayer beads swaying from their clasped hands. The screeching of my gear shifts shattered their serenity. My fitful starts and sudden stops sent them scurrying to safer ground, robes flying, beads rattling. They soon learned to retreat to the motherhouse when my white Ford Galaxy pulled into their lot.

In spite of the nuns' supplications to the Almighty that I pass the driving test and get off their sacred ground, I failed it twice. I yearned to give up, but knew I couldn't. I had to fight my way out of this fear. I was in my thirties the first time I sat behind the wheel of a car. I didn't approach driving with the glee of a teenager who can't wait to get his license and access to his father's wheels. When I finally passed the test, I knew why the caged bird sings. Driving along unfamiliar roads not caring if I was lost, escaping kids, dogs, and Phil, whose foot was always stretching for the brake when I was driving, I exulted in the freedom that Maya Angelou's mournful bird longs for.

An even greater liberation came when I conquered my fear of flying. This was an almost insurmountable challenge, but once overcome, it opened doors that all my life had been closed to me. That leap out of a paralysis triggered by fear was not a bold act of courage. I had made many false starts, buying plane tickets and canceling them at the last minute as anxiety, then panic set in. When I finally took the plunge, in my forties, it was not on a puddle-jumper flight to Miami. I accompanied Phil on a business trip across the country, from New York to San Francisco. That first flight set me free to experience places I had only dreamt about. I could now speak my college French in France. I could cook in Tuscany, shop the marketplaces in Provence. I could tell the time by counting the tolls of Big Ben in London. Phil was right; though it came many years later than my girlhood false start, traveling in Europe did change my life.

Had I not overcome my fear of flying, I would not have been able to start a new life, late in life, in San Francisco. Making the decision to relocate wasn't easy. I would be leaving Amy and her children, which was the only entry in the con column on our yellow pad when we were debating the move, but it was an agonizing one. I still wrestle with it. I would also be leaving friends of many years; how would I make new friends at this late age? I no longer had young children whose friends' mothers would become my friends. I no longer had a dog to walk and chat with other pet lovers. I no longer had a job and co-workers with common interests.

I had been retired for ten years, at peace with the idea of comfortably living out my remaining years in the suburb where we raised our children. The highlight of my summer days was sitting on the porch, waiting for Phil to finish his gardening chores and bring me a vodka tonic in a frosted glass. Frigid winter days were spent reading in front of the fire, my poodle nestled in beside me. Why would I leave this house, so filled with memories of young children and puppies growing up together? Where sixteen people squeezed around a table meant for twelve at Thanksgiving, everyone talking at once, the sound of laughter filling the air? I didn't know then that I would carry that life's music with me wherever I went. I didn't know that taking that risk would give me a future at a time when I thought my life was all about the past. Instead of being surrounded by loved ones as I blew out candles on my 75th birthday, I was on an American Airlines flight somewhere between the East and West coasts, not knowing what this new life would bring.

The Transition

Dear Karen,

I've been out of touch for a very long time, for a very good reason. In March, Phil and I decided to move to San Francisco, and in August, the move was a *fait accompli!* Once we made our decision (a very emotional one, since we left our daughter and her family, including my darling Leah), the move went lightning fast. We've always loved San Francisco, been visiting for fifteen years. You may remember we have a son and two grandchildren here. So we made one child happy, and left one quite sad.

We went from a house in the suburbs to an apartment in a high rise building in the Financial District. We're within walking distance of the Embarcadero, the Ferry Building and its Plaza that has a wonderful greenmarket and craft fare every weekend. It's like being on vacation all the time. And the weather, after New York's blizzards and summer's relentless humidity, has been blissful.

Dear Susie,

Truth is, it was hard for me to imagine myself living in a high rise building. I have never lived in anything but a house, with a stint in a second-floor garden apartment—but I love that part of our "great adventure," as people insist on calling it. Initially, I was upset at the way other residents nod in the elevator, then disappear behind closed doors. But some of those barriers are coming down. I'm finding that, if I put myself at risk by saying "hello" first, the responses are warming up. I've never considered saying "hello" a risk.

October 2005

Dear Anita,

I'm coming to terms with the fact that my daughter is now 3,000 miles away, and that I will never have both children on the same coast. I'm no longer grieving over that, but still mourning. (Joan Didion put me on to the difference between the two.)

Dear Debbie,

I'm doing my best to accept the move. I'm almost convinced that this is where we should be at this point in our lives and trying to enjoy the undeniable pleasures of this city, one of which, for Uncle Phil, is the year-round presence of flowers, which compensates for the loss of his own garden. He's really happy here. He's traded in his New York driver's license for a California one. I'm not ready to do that yet.

Leaving our home of so many years was made easier because we're very fond of the young couple who bought it. They love the house and keep writing to tell us so. We just learned she's expecting a baby. It's comforting to know there will once again be a nursery at 19 Justamere Drive.

December 2005

Dear Messue and Ken,

What a hectic time this has been for us. We were hardly back from Thanksgiving in New York when I plunged full steam ahead into Christmas preparations for Amy and her family—their first visit to our new home. We had Christmas Eve here in the apartment and I was careful to have all the special foods I used to make for Bob when he came home to NY for the holidays. We had a live tree, trimmed with everybody's special ornaments (I knew what NOT to sell at the moving sale!). And though the apartment is much smaller than the house, I found a place to display every decoration the kids

ever made for me. My mother was right about the holidays—
you really have to work at making them happy.

Christmas Day was at Bob's house where, miraculously, all
the wrapped gifts I'd been sending over there for weeks were
under the tree. His wife made *lumpia*, Filipino hors d'oeuvres.
We lit candles in a menorah and said the prayers every night of
Hanukkah that Amy was here. Don't ask me who I am at this
point. And what would my mother think?

January 2006

Dear Elaine,

We went to Lake Tahoe after Christmas for some much-
needed R&R. The day we arrived, weather reports began to be
ominous, two to three feet of snow were predicted, which
would close the roads for who knows how long. Bob decided
we should leave that evening.

The first part of the trip would take us down a snow-
covered mountain. Remembering all the hair-pin turns coming
up, my vote on whether or not we should leave was no, but I
was overruled. Chains were put on the tires and we started
down as a blizzard began to blow. When we stopped at a
service station to ask about conditions, we were told, "Not a
good night to be on the mountain." I held my breath all the
way down.

The joke, now that we're all breathing out again, is:
Wouldn't it have been ironic if we left New York because of
the weather, came to sunny California, and died in a
blizzard?

April 2006

Dear Eleanor,

Amy just called and Leah got on the phone. We had a long talk about her coming Bat Mitzvah, what she's studying, wearing, etc. She has it all under control. You can't imagine the amount of preparation this event requires. I'm attaching a note from Amy and my response, to give you an idea of the whirl everyone's in, on both coasts.

Mom,

I have spent more money trying to pull myself together for this event. I have to tell you, you don't realize what a mess you are normally until something like this comes up.

Amy,

You'll get no sympathy from me. Can you imagine what it takes to pull a 70-something ruin together? More important than the money is the timing—when should I get my hair colored, my nails manicured, my eyebrows waxed, my dress altered? Not to mention that I need a heroic strapless bra to lift my boobs off my lap, industrial strength Spanx to pull in my stomach, and a magic bolero to hide my unsightly arms. And I'm just the grandmother.

August 2006

Dear Cathie,

What a happy week I had with my two girls. Leah and Jenna are two years apart, and they are great together in spite of how rarely they see each other; so many miles between them.

Leah had a hair-straightening device which she used every day to no avail once she stepped out into the morning fog. Jenna, whose hair is stick-straight, is now sleeping with rollers because she wants hair like Leah's.

October 2006

Dear Eleanor,

I spent a whole day with Leah when I was home last month, just the two of us. She wanted to drive by our house, which we did, twice. Then she wanted to walk around the reservoir and we did three laps, like we used to. I asked her if she'd like a manicure and she said, "Actually, I could use a pedicure." After that we went to the pizza place she and I used to escape to. She needed to revisit all the places that were part of her life for so long. So did I.

December 2006

Dear Susie,

Well, here it is Christmas again, our second in San Francisco. The city is beautifully decorated, there's music everywhere, the ice-skating rink on the Plaza is going full-tilt, tourists and locals are in a shopping frenzy. But that damn sun is out all the time, warming us when what I really want is a frosty nip in the air and bushes dripping icicles, not flowers. A fresh snowfall and a blazing fireplace would be nice, too, with my children and grandchildren gathered around it. Christmas is when I yearn for my old home.

Passages

" Aaron, will you come with me to visit the World Trade Center Memorial?" I asked my grandson. I was calling from San Francisco a week before I would leave for New York for his high school graduation. I knew my bonding time with him was coming to an end; he would soon be setting out to seek his own path in life and there would be little time for chilling with his grandmother.

Aaron is the youngest and most challenging of my four grandchildren. Like all challenging people, he will be heard. It started in the maternity ward at the Putnam Hospital Center in New York, where Phil and I met him soon after he was born. The joy in the hospital room that day was palpable. The newborn lay nestled in his mother's arms, swaddled to his chin, his head covered in the blue cap that announced his gender. Two sets of giddy grandparents stared at him like he was the pot of gold at the end of a rainbow. When we visited the next day, we went straight to the nursery to gaze again upon this miracle that was now a part of our lives. We scanned all the blue caps, but couldn't find ours. "Where's our grandson?" we asked the nurse.

"Oh, he's in the Bad Baby Room," she replied.

"What did he do?" we asked. What could a two-day-old baby do that called for punishment, we wondered.

"His crying disturbs the other babies," the nurse answered. "We can't have that now, can we?"

Of course not, I thought. That rarity, a crying infant, simply had to be removed from all those conformists in their pink and blue caps who nursed and burped, then slept until it was time to nurse and burp again. Aaron was having none of it. From day two of his life, he's been doing his own thing, in his own way, on his own time.

Eighteen years later, on the plane to New York, I thought about the baby, the boy, and now the young man I was on my way to meet. Though he had readily agreed to come to the 9/11 museum, I wondered how much he remembered of that day, and recalled my own memories of that tragedy's unfolding.

The day started out bright and sunny. I was in a sunny frame of mind, too. I was beginning to feel optimistic after surgery for breast cancer. The prognosis was good; I would live, after all. Life was looking up again. Then the phone rang. "Mom, put TV on, there's been a terrible accident in the city."

It was Amy calling from her suburban New York home to mine. She stayed on the phone and, together, we watched a replay of a plane crashing into the North Tower of the World Trade Center, an image that, sixteen years later, is still vivid in my mind. While trying to grasp the horror of the first crash, we witnessed another plane dive deliberately into the South Tower, and we knew for certain that the first crash had not been an accident.

During my recuperation, I read about the healing powers of laughter and I chose to believe it. Laughter has always come easily for me. Unlike the weeks of radiation treatments I was enduring, this was a remedy I would enjoy. But as I sat numb in front of television that day and watched first one tower, then the other crumble like sandcastles before my eyes, I felt I would never laugh again. My niece Lisa was in one of those towers.

It was drizzling lightly when Aaron and I left home. The only umbrella in Amy's house was child-sized; playful puppies frolicked over its plastic span. I had bought it for Leah when she entered kindergarten. When we emerged from Grand Central Station, there was a steady downpour and that inappropriate umbrella saved the day. There wasn't a cab to be had. "Don't worry, Nana," Aaron said. "We'll take the subway." I hadn't ridden the New York City subway in many years and had no idea how to get so far downtown.

"I don't know which line to take," I said.

"Follow me."

We descended into an underground teeming with people who knew where they were going and which train to take to get there. They swept past us, poured through the turnstiles, and crushed into already packed cars. Used to San Francisco's comparatively miniscule Muni system, I was overwhelmed. Aaron took charge. He read the signs and studied the transit maps, then he led me to the train that would take us to the Memorial.

There was no way to avoid a drenching when we got there. It was a two-block walk to the site in torrential rain. On the way, Aaron spotted one of those hotdog carts ubiquitous on the streets of New York. Since he was a toddler, he'd loved what he called "franks in dirty water." These were hotdogs that had been sitting in greasy water made even less wholesome by the city air, alive with debris and noxious fumes from the gridlocked street traffic. It was hotdog heaven to Aaron when he was a child, and he had to have one now.

"Oh, Aaron, grow up," I said.

But he insisted, and went off to get one. I ran under a construction awning for shelter from the rain. When I looked back, I noticed the "Sabrett" logo on the vendor's umbrella. A Sabrett pushcart hotdog is one of those foods, like pizza, that ex-New Yorkers yearn for but can't be replicated anywhere else. It's a top-of-the-line sidewalk frank. The quality of the water it sits in simply is not an issue. I left the shelter of the awning and ran to the corner, trying to get Aaron's attention. The wind had its way with my toy umbrella and I had to close it. Passing cars, swishing through puddles, splashed me all over. But I didn't care, I was on a nostalgic mission.

"Aaron," I shouted, "Get me one, too."

When we arrived at Ground Zero, there was no refuge from the rain. We went through the security checkpoints, standing in long, solemn lines. The Memorial pools are set in the two footprints where the Twin Towers had once dominated the Manhattan skyline. Thirty-foot waterfalls cascade into their centers. The names of all the victims, 2,977 killed in 2001 and 6 killed in the 1993 attack on the Towers, are etched in bronze around the perimeter of the pools. Our mission this day was to find Lisa's name.

We were puzzled when we saw that the names are not arranged alphabetically, but learned that, honoring requests from the victims' families for specific names to be in the same area, they reflect where the victims were on 9/11 and the working relationships they had shared with others who were lost that day. An electronic directory at the site made it easy for us to find Lisa. It told us she had worked in the South Tower and her name was on Panel S-36.

We sloshed our way to the South pool, Aaron taking the lead. My glasses were so beaded with raindrops, I could hardly see ahead, much less read the names. "Don't worry, Nana," Aaron said. "I'll find her." When he did, we stood silently, two generations removed from each other, equally mesmerized by a name cast in bronze.

Aaron was five years old when Lisa died. Though he'd heard stories of her loss on that terrible day, before this visit to the Memorial, he had little memory of her. The electronic directory that led us to her name also had a picture of her, a young woman in a flowered summer dress, her unruly blond hair framing a pretty smile. "I remember her!" Aaron said, "That's Katie's mother." Lisa had become real for him.

Standing beside him, my mind called up indelible images of the day and its aftermath. I remembered that we went to the city the day after the attack to be with Eleanor; Lisa was her daughter-in-law. It was a time when Americans everywhere felt a vulnerability we had never known before. We needed to be with loved ones; we needed to assure each other that we would get through this. Calls were made across the country asking, "Are you all right?" even of those who were not in harm's way during the attack, but whose lives would be changed forever because of it. As we drove the West Side Highway, a busload of firefighters on their way to Ground Zero to join in the search for survivors came into view. Every car in its path pulled to the side of the road to clear the way. We saluted them silently as they went by; they, in turn, pressed the palms of their hands against the windows of the bus to acknowledge our thanks.

The umbrella Aaron held offered no protection in the driving rain, but he held it resolutely over my head. I wept tears of loss for this young mother who went to work one day and never came home. I wept tears of pride for this young man who had spent this day helping me find my way. I knew that we had each crossed into another of life's passages; I was now in his care.

For the first time that day, I wasn't distressed by the weather. It seemed a fitting backdrop for so sad a journey. The rain, the waterfalls, the tears— it was a wet day all around.

Remembering The Times I Was Happy

If I remember the times I was happy, maybe they will keep me from dwelling on the dark days. One of the darkest of all came late in my life. I doubt there is time enough left to fully recover from it, but I make small gains every day. I try to be gentle with myself, to not expect too much. Abraham Lincoln said, *"Every man is as happy as he wants to be."* Assuming that applies to women, too, I've re-set my goal and now aim for content instead of happy. Content is more attainable; I've made a soft landing there and I've stopped reaching for what can no longer be.

This has freed me to remember the times I was happy and, on a good day, even to re-capture their essence. They came at different ages, during different periods of my life. I remember graduating from college, so optimistic about what lay ahead, so naively unaware that the ladder of life goes down, as well as up.

I remember getting my first writing job at Parents' magazine, located across the street from Grand Central Station in Manhattan where my commuter train from Brooklyn deposited me each morning. My world became much wider when I left the borough of churches and embraced the city of dreams. I was so ready for the excitement it offered. Newly arrived, I learned to pick up my pace or be knocked down by the rushing masses on the sidewalks; wherever they were going, it was always at breakneck speed. My lunch hour was not just for eating, I had to get to Lord & Taylor's department store and back without being late. I was learning how to dress, too. I became adept at beating the traffic lights on Fifth Avenue between 42nd Street, where I worked, and 38th Street, where Lord & Taylor was; if I made the first green light, I would make them all. Office parties were held at restaurants where I first ate the food that would have a lifelong influence on my taste buds, and later would send me to its place of origin, again and again. When I was introduced to *pommes soufflés* at a bistro around the corner from my office, my life as a Francophile began. It was an exciting time of beginnings all around for me. This is when I began my writing life, and when I met the man I would marry.

I remember going with him to the Cloisters, a branch of the Metropolitan Museum of Art dedicated to the art and architecture of medieval Europe. The museum overlooks the Hudson River in northern Manhattan. No ruins here; the aging stone arches we strolled under, impeccably preserved, were framed in the brilliant foliage of a northeastern autumn. The bright yellows and vibrant reds of leaves still clinging to life rivaled the splendor of the art. We stood awed before the statuary and tapestries, and lingered in the terraced gardens. But the greatest wonder, for us, was our being there together. Of all the things we discovered that day, the most important was each other. We never stopped talking on the Fifth Avenue bus ride all the way down to Grand Central Station, on the way home and on the way to a life together.

I remember moving to the hamlet of Hartsdale, New York, as a bride and learning, too late, that a hamlet is not a city, it's not a town, it's not even a village—it's a settlement. I had left life in a metropolis for life in a settlement. I woke each morning asking myself, *What am I doing here?* Like Goldie Hawn's Private Benjamin, I wanted to wear sandals, I wanted to go to lunch, I wanted my old life back. When I brought my infant daughter home to that settlement, it no longer mattered where I lived, as long as she was there.

I remember the first time I got lost in Paris. I always declared on-my-own days when we traveled. I'd pretend I was that young girl who almost took a solo trip to Europe so long ago. With no tour escort to guide me and no husband to lead the way, I was free to experience the elation of going my own way, making my own discoveries. This day, my destination was Place de la Concorde on the Right Bank to see where Marie Antoinette had met her fate at the guillotine, and to thank her for provoking the revolution that created the France I love. I was looking for Pont Royal, my usual crossing to the Right Bank, when I found myself in front of a Left Bank architectural landmark. It was Musee d'Orsay, home to the most extensive collection of Impressionist art in the world. I dismissed all thoughts of Marie Antoinette and spent the afternoon with the Impressionists instead. I wandered through gallery after gallery, pausing when I came to Renoir's *Two Sisters*. I sat on a bench before it for a long while, wishing Eleanor was there beside me. Renoir was her favorite Impressionist. She loved this painting best because it reminded her of the two of us.

I had seen many of these works in other museums at home and abroad. But here I was in the Impressionists' home town, the very place where they had created these masterpieces. I walked the streets they had walked, those bearded, often shabby citizens of Paris who left a legacy for the ages. I came away feeling a personal connection with them. Getting lost has led to some of my most memorable travel experiences. Like John Steinbeck, *"I'm never upset at being lost, and I take no pleasure in being found."*

I remember when my granddaughter Jenna announced a week before my birthday, "You're going to like my gift best." She delighted in finding the perfect gift for the people she loved. She had talked the family into going to Portland, Oregon, so I could visit Powell's, the world's largest independent book store. From the time I learned that it occupies an entire city block and is home to a million books, I had wanted to go. She understood because she's a bookworm, too. We were given two hours to immerse ourselves in this world that we loved before the family would return and take us away. We browsed randomly, we searched for our favorite authors, we read the flaps of more books than we had ever seen in one place. When we left, Powell's had one million books, minus two. Jenna bought one for me for my birthday; I bought one for her because I always bought her books. I became a Jane Austen fan later in life than most, but when I fell, I fell hard and became a collector. I chose *Sense and Sensibility* for my birthday book. I cherish it, and keep it near. On days when the darkness descends, I pick it up, open it to any chapter, and I am back at Powell's on that magical afternoon, just the two of us, awash in a sea of books.

Use The Good Stuff

I was raised by a mother who taught us to save things "for good." That included everything we didn't need to survive the current day. I carried that mantra through much of my life—not using china I loved except for a special occasion; not wearing that new outfit today because I might receive an invitation to lunch tomorrow; keeping the last tube of a lipstick whose shade has been discontinued for "special," instead of looking my best when I have coffee alone at Starbucks.

Going through my mother's things when she died, I found gifts my siblings and I had given her over the years—scarves, gloves, jewelry—still in their boxes, wrapped in yellowing tissue, waiting for an occasion important enough to wear them.

Erma Bombeck, the humorist who wrote about suburban home life, did this, too. When she was diagnosed with a fatal illness, she wrote a column titled, *If I Had My Life to Live Over,* listing what she would do differently in life if she was granted the chance to do it all over again.

The last item is one I try to keep in mind:

Mostly, given another shot at life, I would seize every minute … really see it … live it.

I, too, have regrets about things that could have been and never will be. Unlike Erma Bombeck, I have been granted another shot at life; I survived my cancer. But after a lifetime of making tomorrow more important than today, I sometimes have to force myself to take that shot. My mother is in part to blame for this. Never underestimate the tenacity of a mother's teachings. I've outlived my mother by many years, I've surpassed her in formal learning, I function in a technology-driven world that she never could have coped with. Yet her simple lessons and cautions still influence my every day.

For Christmas dinner two years ago, I surprised my family with a new appetizer, Japanese Rumaki. Whole water chestnuts are wrapped in bacon that has been spread with brown sugar on one side, and whole-grain dijon mustard on the other. The bacon is secured with a toothpick and the wraps are baked until the bacon is crisp. Everyone liked them, but Jenna loved them. "Nana, promise you'll make them again!"

"Next occasion," I promised.

Jenna didn't have a next occasion, and I never got to keep that promise. Getting through holidays without her is painful. The can of water chestnuts that I bought and saved just for her sits in my cupboard. I will never use it. It's there to remind me that life itself is a special occasion. It's also a symbol of a regret that will always haunt me. When I am tempted to save for tomorrow something that would make me happy today I think of that unopened can of water chestnuts. Use the good stuff, I tell myself. Don't wait for that perfect moment. It's now.

Benvenuto, Guiseppe!

My grandson Joe, a recent college graduate, is taking a long look at this world, trying to define his place in it. I understand where he's at, and I'm happy that he doesn't have to make a decision that he's not yet ready to make. As my mother told me, "You'll need more than dreams; you'll need a job," Joe's mother also feels he should be taking his first steps towards his life's work. I always agree with her, but whisper to myself, *Don't rush into anybody's life but yours, Joe.*

It seems only yesterday that I first learned there would be another Joe in my life. We were standing on the banks of the Bay in Sausalito eating ice cream cones and enjoying the view of the San Francisco skyline when Bob and his girlfriend announced their engagement. This was followed by a second announcement: They would name their first son Joseph, after my father. The young couple's intentions brought tears to my eyes.

My father has always been my hero. Born into poverty in Italy, at the age of 10 he was sent across the ocean by his mother to establish roots in the New World. His story validates the adage: *Success is measured not by where you are, but by how far you've come.* Using that as a yardstick, my father is the biggest success story I know.

Always in awe of the education he didn't have himself, he was proud of everything his children achieved in school. He was a live-in cheerleader for all of us. When I began writing as a student, then as a professional, he would ask, "Why don't you write the story of our family?" I would reply, "Oh, Dad, who'd want to read it?" I should have written it earlier, if just for him. This is one for my regrets column.

My mother, though born in America was raised in the customs and teachings of her immigrant parents. My maternal grandfather died before I was born, but my grandmother, who went on to live more of her lifetime in America than she had in Italy, never assimilated into the life of the New World. She never learned to speak English and all eight of her children were taught Italian at home and English in school. Having struggled to learn new subjects in a new language, my mother wanted her children to have an easier time. English was the only language spoken in our home; none of us learned the Italian she spoke to her mother and her sisters. She maintained her Italian ways, but she sent her children out into the world as Americans.

As teenagers, Eleanor and I were committed to the Americanization of our mother, who loved this country but held fast to her Old World ways and her tightly-coiled bun. We decided that, to bring Mom up to par with our Irish friends' mothers, the bun had to go. Using preparing for my brother's wedding as an excuse, we talked her into coming to the beauty parlor with us, an alien environment for her. While there, we talked her into being shorn of the bun she had worn all her adult life. With each lock of hair that fell to the floor, some of the essence of who she was drained out of her. But Eleanor and I, insensitive to her loss, were delighted with the results of the cut. "You look like a real American now, Mom," we said. What we didn't understand was, that had never been my mother's goal. She always knew who she was and she was content with that image. She felt ever after that her inner self had been swept away on the floor of "Connie's Cuts— No Appointment Needed."

When I married and moved to the suburbs, I carried Americanization even further in raising my children. None of us spoke Italian at home and neither Amy nor Bob chose Italian as their required foreign language in high school. The most Italian thing about us was we all loved pasta.

Thanksgiving, the quintessential American celebration, has always been my favorite holiday. I love gathering family around the table and serving the tradition-bound foods of the day. I've adopted the trappings of the New England Thanksgiving season. Indian corn hangs on my front door; a jaunty pumpkin, stem askew, sits at the entrance, another is

127

baked in pies. Candied yams and cranberry sauce are staples on my holiday table. I have a set-in-stone Thanksgiving menu rule that my children have had to live with from their earliest years.

"Mommy, this year can we have pasta?" my toddler son, legs dangling through the openings in the supermarket cart, would ask as we shopped for the holiday. "Did the Pilgrims have pasta at the first Thanksgiving?" I would ask. Not waiting for an answer, I'd go into my Thanksgiving mantra: "If the Pilgrims didn't have it, we're not having it." Which, of course, ruled out pasta.

In a moment of weakness, Phil and I agreed to let Bob go to college in California, where he was seduced by the good life and the lovely Filipina girl he announced his engagement to that day in Sausalito. They married and settled in San Francisco. After years of trying unsuccessfully to lure them back East, we joined them in the West. Since then we've been celebrating Thanksgiving at their house. At our first holiday gathering there, we came together with the Filipino family, some of whom had brought a dish to the meal, as I had—my turkey stuffing, whose recipe hasn't changed one whit in three generations. When we were called to the table that first year, I didn't recognize much of the food. There were Filipino egg rolls called *lumpia*, there was a casserole that someone told me is the national dish of the Philippines. Standing with my mouth open, ready to exclaim, "There was no Chicken Adobo at the first Thanksgiving!" I glanced at Phil and saw the panic in his eyes, imploring me silently, "Please—don't give your Pilgrim speech."

Back to the recent college graduate. I think of Joe as being on a detour right now. After many years of being guided, if not nudged, in one direction, he's exploring other possibilities. From his earliest days, Joe has not been afraid to try a different route. When he and Jenna were in pre-school, their mother had to be away for a week and I went to San Francisco to take care of them. One of my responsibilities that week was driving the children to school. One day, on the way home, Joe said, "Nana, sometimes Mommy stops for ice cream after school."

"What a good idea," I said, "But I don't know where the ice cream store is."

"I do," Joe declared firmly.

"Tell me, where is it?"

"It's on the other side of here," he replied just as firmly.

We didn't find his mother's ice cream store that day, but we drove and we searched until we found our own. That's what Joe is doing now, searching for his own place in life. Every day, he is getting closer to finding his side of here.

On the brink of manhood, Joe reminds me of myself at his age, noncommittal, uncommunicative, the quiet one in noisy surroundings. Maybe he is our next generation's writer, the one I've been waiting for. He chose Italian as his required foreign language in college, which came as a complete surprise to me. I first learned about it when he began addressing his emails to me *Cara Nonna,* and signing them *Guiseppe.* As he searches for his own way, my half Filipino grandson is helping me find my way back to my Italian heritage. *Grazie Guiseppe!*

But For The Book

According to family lore, I learned to read before I learned to talk. My mother used to say I was born reading. How else could she explain a kid who would rather sit in the house with a book than be out roller skating or skipping rope with her friends? For all my mother's angst about my doing too much reading and getting not enough fresh air, the book has served me well.

If, indeed, I was born a reader, it's just as certain I was not born an athlete. I was surrounded by siblings and cousins for whom a ball was right up there with the bread of life. For them, a new season was defined not by the weather, but by what sport was played at that time of year. Afternoons, boys rushed home from school, gathered sticks and balls and each other and played in the street until the light faded and they were called in for supper.

Though I loved school, I hated gym, and I hated team sports most of all. I could neither hit nor catch a ball. I couldn't run either; if by chance my bat did connect with a pitch, I never made it to first base. In volleyball and badminton, I couldn't get the ball or the bird over the net. Memoir writers through the ages have told of the scars they bore because they weren't chosen for a team. I bear no scars, I carry no grudges. I wouldn't have picked me, either.

In my family, as in most large families, each child was defined by an attribute. Joe was smart, Lou was the athlete, Rose the dancer, and Eleanor the redhead. I was the reader. Everyone else read, too, but my father's daily newspaper was something he had to get through, while a book was something I didn't want to end. Nor did my siblings read with the intensity I did. Reading didn't take them to another place where they, too, breathed the same Alpine air that *Heidi* did. It didn't take them to the craggy coast of Yorkshire and the mist on the moors where they, too, grieved for Heathcliff and Cathy's ill-fated love in *Wuthering Heights*. They read because it was an option; I read as if my life depended on it. As it turned out, it did.

It was reading that led me to writing, and writing has helped me cope with life's traumas. When faced with a sadness, often I'll put my feelings down on paper and I'm able to move on. When my three-year-old nephew died of leukemia, I had a hard time accepting it. Each morning I woke to a grief that was fresh. Finally I wrote a story about Anthony Nicholas. With a name like that, he's destined for greatness, I had predicted for my brother's newborn son. When that joy turned into inconsolable grief, I did my weeping on paper and put the story in a cabinet I rarely used. If I happened to go by it without thinking, I'd stop short, and back away. My story, and my sorrow, remained sealed in an envelope in that cabinet until my pain subsided.

But for the book, my social life would be a wasteland. Like me, most of my friends are readers. I met them in book clubs, in the bookstore where I work, at the publications for whom I review books. When I find myself in an environment lacking in book people, I wonder how I will cope with the demands of conversation that social events require. Last summer I was invited to my niece's wedding in North Carolina. This would be my first exposure to Southern life and Southern women— who can chat easily on any topic, anytime, anywhere. They are innately gracious and hospitable. I am in awe of them. Born and raised in the North and an introvert at heart, conversation with strangers has never been my forté.

Southern life is very social; a wedding is not a one-day event. Days of partying would precede and follow Meghan's walk down the aisle. Each occasion would require a suitable ensemble and I shopped for weeks putting them together, then had a runway fashion show in my living room for my family, who sat four abreast on the couch as I paraded by. "I don't understand why you're so uptight about this, Nana," Jenna said. "You always look nice." I didn't know how to tell her that "nice" wouldn't do for these occasions. Or, that my being uptight wasn't about the clothes. Did I want her to know that my vulnerability was based on a lack of self confidence? I grew up in a time when the popular image of women was based on perfect hair, perfect body, perfect clothes, all of which were unattainable goals for me. After years of trying to be who I wasn't, I accepted who I was, and became content with the woman I am. Until I was faced with the prospect of coming together with Southern women, who do fit that image. Here I am, ratting myself out again.

I got off to a bad start at the first festivity. It was the Ladies' Luncheon at The Club, where I was the only one wearing pants, dressy pants, but still, mine were the only covered legs in the room. This was followed by a Gathering hosted by the groom's parents welcoming us to the family, and to Charlotte's gracious way of life. Finally, before the wedding celebration itself, there was the Rehearsal Dinner. Though I had done my best to fit sartorially into Charlotte, at all these occasions there was no denying I was dressed for San Francisco, where fitting in is not an issue.

At the Rehearsal Dinner I was seated between the grandfather of the groom, a retired doctor and patriarch of the large family my niece was marrying into, and the groom's aunt, an aloof woman who had traveled from Venice, where she lived, to attend the wedding. Why, I wondered, had my niece chosen me for this challenge? Where is it written that a woman may not be seated next to her husband at a social event? Who makes these rules? Are they cultural? Geographic? Does the wedding planner have the power of the place card, arbitrarily seating 100 guests next to people they don't know?

I turned to the doctor on my right and began a conversation with what I thought was the only thing we had in common, I asked about his retirement. When he mentioned that he volunteers his medical services in needy regions of Africa, I came to life. "There's a book you should read," I said. "Have you heard of *Cutting for Stone*? It's by a doctor and about doctors who practice in Africa."

Just as excited, he replied, "I bought that book last week; haven't started it yet. You say it's good?" And we were off on a lively book talk.

Having overcome the hurdle of the grandfather on my right, I turned to the aunt on my left, and said, "My favorite mystery series takes place in Venice. Have you read any of Donna Leon's Commissario Brunetti books?" She had! We launched into an exchange of favorite titles and characters. I told her I was in awe of Brunetti's wife, the lovely Paola, daughter of a Count, raised in a palace, now teaching literature at university level while raising two teenagers and making home a haven for her beleaguered husband—all of whom come home for lunch. "And it's always a gourmet pasta!" I exclaimed.

"The peanut butter and jelly sandwich has no place on the Italian table," my friend, the Aunt, said. By the time we had exhausted the subject, dessert had been served and it was time to leave.

My husband, more than anyone, knows the part that reading has played in my life. A patient man, he's been waiting more than fifty years for me to close the book. He put a *New Yorker* cartoon that sums up my reading life on the refrigerator door. It shows a man telling a funeral director what he wants done with his deceased wife's remains. The caption reads: *"Bury her nose in a book, and cremate the rest of her."*

Family Trees

I first met Francie Nolan when we were both thirteen and both living in Brooklyn, she in the pages of Betty Smith's novel, *A Tree Grows in Brooklyn*, I in a real-life Brooklyn, both our families struggling through the dark days of the Great Depression. I met her again recently when I watched a television airing of the movie based on the book. I don't often cry at movies, but I wept throughout this one. The characters in the drama unfolding on screen were so like the family in my own childhood that, for two nostalgic hours, I was with them again.

The story of the Irish-American family coping with hard times is told in Francie's wistful voice. Its heroic fictional characters, like the characters in my reality, were poor in material things, but rich in relationships. They survived because they had each other.

Francie is a hard worker like her mother, and a dreamer like her father. Her love of reading provides an escape from the hardships around her. When we first meet her, she is reading her way through her local library; she's finished the A's and is starting on the B's. In another scene, we see her sitting on the fire escape of her tenement flat, lost in a book, oblivious to the hawking of street vendors below and the shouting of hard-pressed neighbors all around her. She is in another place; through her reading and writing she creates better worlds than the one she lives in.

Francie's mother, Katie Nolan, is the strength in this family; she earns the money that supports them by scrubbing floors. She can't depend on her husband Johnny, a singing waiter who rarely finds work. A lovable alcoholic, drunk with drink but also with dreams, Johnny is Francie's hero. They tell each other their dreams and, though he knows his won't come true, he encourages Francie to believe that hers will. Katie doesn't have time for dreams, it's she who puts food on the table and shoes on her children's feet. My mother didn't put any store in dreams, either. "You'll need jobs, not dreams," she told us. My father, a hard-working Italian immigrant, is the one who put shoes on our feet. In addition to his daytime job, he worked two nights a week in Benny's Shoe Store; he was paid in shoes for his family. In spite of the hard times, he never stopped believing that all things are possible in America. I grew up driven by that same dream.

Watching Katie scrub the halls of their tenement on her knees, tenants coming and going tramping over her just-washed floors, brought me back to the chore Eleanor and I hated the most—the Saturday morning cleaning of the halls in our four-story brownstone. I swept the floors and dusted the wooden balusters, one by one; when I was finished, Eleanor mopped the steps and the landings. We had a tenant family on the top floor, the antiseptic Karpuses, a mother with two daughters who were exact replicas of her. Dressed in their somber gray dresses and veiled caps, they attended religious services every Saturday morning without fail, interrupting my sweeping as they descended, and making their return ascent as Eleanor was doing the mopping. They were impervious to her scowls as they tracked dirt over her still wet floors. "Who goes to church on Saturdays, *anyway?*" Eleanor would grumble to me. She had another reason for not liking them. Mrs. Karpus, her faced pinched in disapproval, inspected her work on the way up and pointed out places her mop had missed. Then she rapped loudly on our door and issued a complaint to my mother. "Eleanor should get down and use a brush. She's not getting the corners clean."

Formidable as she was, Mrs. Karpus was no match for Eleanor, who wasn't getting on her knees for anyone. Even I didn't bend to the woman's demands. I always swept the landing between the third and second floors as fast as I could. That's where my Grandmother's coffin got stuck on the way down, after being waked in Aunt Grace's living room. Let Mrs. Karpus find dust balls and report me. I wasn't going to spend a minute more there than I had to.

Katie managed the money in her family, as my mother did in mine. Both always short on funds, they knew how to get a nickel's worth for a nickel spent. When Katie sent Francie to the store, she gave her specific instructions on what to ask for and told her to accept nothing less. Watching Francie give her order to the butcher, starting with "Mama says she wants the beef fresh ground..." reminded me of my opening dialogue when I was sent to the market, "My mother said she wants a *nice* head of lettuce." Shopping at my local farmer's market recently, I spotted a head of butter lettuce that was perfection. Cradling it in two hands, I walked it over to Phil and exclaimed, "Isn't this *gorgeous?*" Puzzled by my awe, he said, "It's a head of lettuce." He didn't understand. That head of lettuce would have earned my mother's approval.

There's a minor character in the story who plays a major role in Katie's life, Mr. Barker, the insurance agent who comes each week to collect the ten cent premium for the insurance policy that Katie struggles, but never fails to pay. This is her security against a disaster that could fall any day. After he collects the dime, Mr. Barker delivers the news about family members, whose dimes he also collects weekly. My mother's insurance agent was George, "the Prudential man" we kids used to call him. He went from floor to floor at 410, collecting dimes and delivering news from my grandmother and the one aunt who didn't live in our neighborhood. In effect, he was the phone none of us had.

I've saved my favorite character for last: Aunt Sissy, Katie's sister, who is as flamboyant as Katie is stable. Her vulnerability, put delicately, is that "men liked her too much." She is a free spirit in conventional times. Even though Katie disapproves of

Sissy, she always ends up forgiving her, as my mother did her youngest sister Anna. Francie adores her aunt for the fun she brings to an otherwise drab life, just as I loved my Aunt Anna, who also thumbed her nose at convention and brought laughter with her wherever she went.

Me? I'm Francie, the dreamer who wanted to be a writer.

Poor Aunt Alice

Aunt Alice, married to my mother's brother John, was the only Irish member of our family. She was neither welcomed nor accepted. This is where the aunts turned the table on the Irish who had greeted the later arrival of Italian immigrants with unabated hostility. They used Poor Aunt Alice to settle the score. The one thing that never failed to unite the sisters was their conviction that Aunt Alice was at the root of all the family troubles.

Uncle John did not bring his wife to live with them in Park Slope, but he did make the mistake of buying a two-family house in the Bay Ridge section of Brooklyn with Aunt Susie, the oldest and most domineering of the sisters. She was as round as she was tall and always wore a crocheted cap that covered all her hair. I remember asking my mother if Aunt Susie *had* hair, a question that would have earned Eleanor a smack. Whenever Aunt Susie was coming for a visit, all the children were warned by our mothers to be on our best behavior, and every inch of us was scrubbed, paying special attention to our ears. When Eleanor complained to my mother, "Why does Aunt Susie look in our ears, *anyway?"* she got that smack.

This is the aunt that Poor Aunt Alice was to share a house with—Aunt Susie on the first floor, she on the second. When a Sunday jaunt for my family included a drive to Bay Ridge, it was just to visit Aunt Susie; nobody made the climb to the second floor. I have no memory at all of Aunt Alice's home. When she came to dinner with the family, hers was the only coiffed head among all those homespun buns. She sat in splendid isolation. She was received, she was fed, she was otherwise ignored.

Fast forward a generation. My brother Lou is now engaged to an Irish girl. My mother had reservations about bringing another "Irish" into the family, but she honored Lou's choice. When we met Jane, we liked her, and she liked us. She would have an easier time than Poor Aunt Alice. We were, after all, a more enlightened generation.

A wedding date was set, but there was no talk of the two families meeting which, according to custom, took place at a dinner given by the bride's mother. Jane's family was large; she was one of twelve, all of her siblings brothers. At one time her father had been mayor of Elizabeth, New Jersey, city of oil refineries and noxious odors. Politics was in the blood of all but the requisite priest. In an Irish family, if there are enough sons, one is groomed for the priesthood.

Just weeks away from the wedding, my mother asked Lou when we would meet Jane's family. Lou spoke to Jane and an invitation to dinner was extended by her mother to just my parents. "You have a sister," my mother told Lou. He talked to Jane and the invitation was expanded to include me. I was in college at the time, the only sibling living at home. Going to that dinner was the last thing I wanted. I begged my mother to leave me home, but she insisted I come, I suspect because she needed some Italian support. At this point, none of us was thinking of Lou as Italian.

So, we got in the car and drove to Elizabeth where we were received by every one of Jane's brothers, whose wives had also been invited. The Italian to Irish ratio was overwhelmingly in their favor; no one seemed happy to meet us. It was obvious there would be no blending of families in this marriage. When dinner was served, the matriarch announced, "I didn't go to any trouble; I got chicken pot pies from Howard Johnson." On the way home, my mother, the consummate Italian cook, asked, "What was that we ate?"

I was nineteen years old when I attended that dinner where I wasn't wanted. When I think of the times in my life when I've felt unwelcome, that's the benchmark I use for comparison. Nothing has ever topped it.

The main event was still ahead; invitations to the wedding arrived. Aunt Alice had died but all the other aunts accepted. Having survived the pot pie dinner, my mother, clearly overstepping her bounds, thought an inquiry into the wedding feast was in order. She asked Lou; Lou asked Jane, then called my mother and told her the main dish would be chicken á la king.

"What is that?" she asked.

"It's very good, Mom," Lou replied. "It's chunks of chicken in a cream sauce, with—"

"Your aunts won't eat that," she said definitively, cutting him off. My aunts, like my mother, had never eaten a sauce that wasn't red. Looking back, I wonder why Jane and Lou, hapless messengers caught between two incompatible, antagonistic mothers, didn't just elope.

On the day of the wedding, a single-file caravan of Italian aunts and uncles, my father's Buick in the lead, his ever-present fedora just inches above the wheel, left Brooklyn, crossed the George Washington Bridge, and drove to Elizabeth.

"Che puzza?" ("What stinks?") the aunts asked as they approached the city and were assaulted by its malodorous air. Dressed in their best blacks and browns, they sat on one side of the hotel dining room at the reception eating roast chicken and peas; the Irish relatives, dressed in shades of pastel blue that matched their eyes, sat on the other, eating chicken á la king. There was no music, therefore no dancing; the matriarch didn't approve of either. Fraternization was neither encouraged nor tolerated. Both sides ate quickly, wanting to bring this happy occasion to the soonest possible end. When it was over, the Italians marched to their cars, formed a caravan pointed in the reverse direction, and got out of New Jersey as fast as they could.

Fast forward one more generation. Intermarriage between Irish and Italians is now a common occurrence in our family.

Our Irish relatives are no longer considered out-laws; they are simply family, like the rest of us. Each side finds much to admire in the other and we are all enriched by our differences. I've wondered why this coming together was so difficult for my parents' generation and so easy for my children's. I think the answer is, today's children don't think of themselves as Irish or Italian. They've thrown themselves together, mixed and blended on high speed, and come out American. They've succeeded where previous generations failed.

Poor Aunt Alice. Too bad she didn't live to see it.

R_{ose}

On mornings when I don't have to jump to the sound of the alarm, when I can lie in bed and wake up slowly, I sometimes think of times past. One recent morning, I woke up thinking about Rose, the older of my two sisters. I remembered the day, eighteen years ago, when I knew I was going to lose her.

It was a typical bleak January day in New York, a day that would be well-spent sitting by the fire with a book and a mug of hot chocolate, but I had a mission in Manhattan. There was a scent of snow in the air as I boarded a Metro-North commuter train in White Plains. When I arrived at Grand Central Station, I blended into the echoing mass that flooded the main concourse. I'd made this trip countless times before when I worked in the city, but this day I was there for another reason. I was on my way to Mt. Sinai Hospital to join my family. Rose was scheduled for brain surgery that morning. She had been diagnosed with an inoperable tumor, but had chosen to have the surgery that a second team of doctors had offered as a remote last chance. They had made it clear that the prospect for recovery was not good, but Rose wanted that chance. We would be there to support her. The only way a family can get through something like this, is together.

I stopped at Zaro's Bakery before exiting the station and bought a bag of warm bagels. I was cold. I was scared. I knew everyone gathered in the family comfort room at the hospital would be, too. Maybe warm bagels would help.

There are two years between my sister Eleanor and me. Though we were all in the same family, Eleanor and I lived very separate lives from those of our three much older siblings. Rose was so far ahead of us in age that she was always our older sister, never our childhood friend. We grew up not really knowing her. She was old enough to feel the full impact of the Depression. She worked as a seamstress to help support our struggling family while Eleanor and I struggled with the rules of grammar in Mrs. Babb's elementary school class.

How we envied Rose's social life. Awe-struck kids, we looked on as her friends gathered at our house to dress for weekend parties and do each other's hair. Our role in preparing for the festivities was as errand girls, carrying messages between Rose and her girlfriends; we had no phone, a luxury at the time. The demands on us were especially heavy when a big event was coming up, like the New Year's Eve formal when the dresses were long and the excitement palpable. "Run over to Helen's and tell her to be here no later than eight o'clock. On your way back, stop at Millie's and remind her to bring her curling iron tonight." When the girls gathered, Eleanor and I watched as they got ready, wishing we could wear long dresses and go to the dance. We wanted so much to be a part of it. "Someday we'll be dressing for dances, too," Eleanor assured me.

So we watched, and we waited our turn. It never came. Pearl Harbor was attacked, World War II was declared, and the dancing stopped. Now Rose's friends gathered at our house to knit argyle socks and scarves for their boyfriends overseas. The dances never resumed. They were replaced with weddings for the lucky girls whose soldiers came home.

Rose did things for us, too. My mother put her in charge of our clothing alterations. This consisted mainly of re-sizing dresses and skirts that were bought for a plump Eleanor to fit a skinny kid when they were handed down to me. I hated those fitting sessions. I had to stand on a stool, perfectly still, with Rose on her knees before me, pins in her mouth.

"You're gonna swallow them," I'd say.

"Pull your stomach in!" she'd order, with a swat at my middle.

"Mom, Rose punched me."

"Stand straight and listen to your sister."

Rose was a talented seamstress. She could alter anything, no matter how difficult the task. I always hated sewing. The rite of passage from elementary to high school required the girls to sew their own graduation dresses. They had to be white and they had to be hand-sewn; machine stitching was not allowed. The sewing medal would be awarded to the graduate whose dress had the best hand-stitching. I chose a delicate dotted-Swiss fabric and a McCall's pattern because they were the easiest to use. I laid the material out on the dining room table and pinned the flimsy tissue pieces of the pattern to the fabric and cut around them. For weeks, following instructions, I put my dress together with painstaking, tiny hand stitches. When our dresses were finished, they were judged by a panel of teachers using magnifying glasses. They inspected the seams and consulted each other, then pronounced my stitches the best. I cried all the way home.

"Why are you crying?" my mother asked.

"I won the sewing medal."

"Isn't that good?"

She didn't understand. My stitches were perfect, but the dress fit like a burlap bag. It was at least two sizes too big. I was afraid everyone would laugh when I went up for the award. "I should have made big ugly stitches," I cried. "I never wanted that medal, anyway."

When Rose came home from work that night, she set about fixing the problem. "Stop crying," she said. "Put the dress on and get on the stool." She pinned the dress into shape, then took a scissors and cut out the excess material, including the medal-winning stitches, replacing them with machine-made seams. On graduation day, feeling like a fraud, I marched up to the stage in my perfectly fitting dress and accepted the medal for stitches that no longer existed.

We all came through the Depression and The War, and Eleanor and I grew up along the way. The age gap between us and Rose closed. We were now three sisters, not two.

When I arrived at the hospital clutching my bag of bagels, Eleanor looked up, the fear on her face so unlike the smile she always had for me. Neither she nor I had wanted Rose to have this surgery. There was little hope it would make a difference in her original prognosis and she had suffered so much already. But it was Rose's decision to make. Her adult children, a daughter and two sons, dreading what was about to happen, sat quietly. We waited, none of us speaking, just being there for Rose, and for each other. I sensed the presence of other families who had sat in sorrow on these same wooden chairs in this depressing room that offered no comfort. The bagels, untouched, grew cold.

When, at last, Rose's gurney was wheeled down the long corridor leading to the Operating Room, we all walked beside it. Rose, sedated, couldn't open her eyes. All the way en route to the OR we told her we loved her. She squeezed our hands to tell us she knew we were there, she heard us. We dropped back when the orderlies asked us to, all but her younger son. He gripped his mother's hand until an orderly made him release it by gently unfolding his fingers, one by one. Rose disappeared on the other side of the OR door; we were left standing there, hoping for a miracle, knowing there wouldn't be one.

I would bring her flowers from Phil's garden in her last days. She had survived the surgery and was sent home from

Mt. Sinai Hospital to live out what little time she had left. I wanted her to have beauty in her life as she lay dying. She wouldn't let anyone throw them out, no matter how wilted, until I came with more. One day, there was no one home when I arrived at her house. I sat on the steps outside for hours, daffodils and daisies drooping on my lap, until an ambulance pulled up at the curb with Rose in it. Eleanor, who always accompanied Rose to her treatments, told me later that her face lit up when she saw me.

Though those visits rang with laughter as we re-told childhood stories, they were in reality the saddest times the three of us had ever spent together. It was Eleanor's fierce determination to brighten Rose's last days that gave me the strength to get through them. Rose, always beautiful and rightly vain, removed her head scarf only for us, knowing that Eleanor and I would see her beauty through her baldness.

For many years, Rose and I had lived separate lives. After I left home, we never lived in the same town again. I chose a life that was broader than the one she was happy in, but we came together before the end, and once again closed a gap that had kept us apart.

Life And Love In An Italian Kitchen

I have no childhood memory of my mother sleeping. She went to bed after I did at night and got up before me the next morning to start breakfast and prepare the family for our day at school or work. In my young mind, mothering was a 24-hour-a-day job.

On Sunday, when the rest of us slept in, she was up even earlier than usual, filling the house with what I will always think of as Sunday morning smells. The long process of making the gravy for that day's pasta dinner was an inflexible ritual. It always started with browning cloves of garlic in oil poured from a gallon can with holes in two diagonal corners that my father had punched with an ice pick. Imported olive oil was a staple in our kitchen, purchased from our neighborhood Italian provisions store, a Saturday morning shopping routine for my mother.

When I accompanied her, I would pull the next number from the dispenser and take my place in line beside her. I remember being overwhelmed by the pungent smells of its prepared foods—the golden fried rice balls with mozzarella melting inside, the glistening roasted red peppers with anchovies and black olives. I would stand in awe before shelves heavy with imported pastas in every shape—long and thin, tubes and squares, squiggles and bows. I stared, mesmerized, at the bearded man in the long white apron behind the deli counter as he sliced pricey prosciutto so thin it was almost translucent, tenderly placing the slices between sheets of waxed paper. I held my nose at the cheese bins, but that's where I learned that the worse a cheese smells, the better it tastes. This Mecca for serious Italian cooks was a vestige of life in the old country carried to the new and passed down to generations of children who still honor it. No matter how Americanized we've become, our cheese is still from Parma; our tomatoes, while no longer preserved at home, are canned in Italy and cross the Atlantic to our tables.

Back to Sunday morning. When the garlic released its essence, its work was done but my mother's work at the stove was just beginning. She removed the garlic from the pot and added a diced onion. Wakened by the first whiffs of garlic and onion, I'd remember it was Sunday and join her in the kitchen. She assembled the essential meats. Links of pork sausage and fleshy spare ribs, each with its own flavor and spicy aroma, were lightly browned in the oil and removed from the pot. Jars of crushed tomatoes, preserved at home the previous summer by my mother and her sisters, their hands and aprons stained red for days, were poured into the pot. Fresh basil leaves from my father's garden and a generous sprinkle of grated Parmesan cheese were added. The meat was returned to the pot; the pot was covered. The scene was set for the next stage—the hours-long simmering on low heat, carefully watched and stirred to prevent burning.

At this point, my mother would step away from the stove and set the table for breakfast. Only then did she allow herself to sit with a cup of coffee. But not for long; it was time to make the meatballs. All the ingredients—ground meats, eggs, breadcrumbs, cheese—were measured into a bowl and squished together with her sturdy hand until the mixture turned a bright pink and bore no lumps.

"Can I do the squishing?" I'd ask.

She would reply, "You're not ready yet."

I didn't know what that meant at the time. But she did show me how to roll the meat into balls between the palms of my hands. Standing side by side at the kitchen table, we'd roll all the mixture, placing the balls on a platter. I counted them every time, and every time there were sixteen.

"Stand back from the stove," she'd say, so I wouldn't be burned by splattering oil as she dropped the balls, evenly spaced, into a heavy frying pan, blackened with use and age, one of her treasured cooking utensils. The immediate sizzle and pop, followed by compelling aromas, woke the whole family. I defy anyone to sleep through the frying of meatballs.

My husband, also of Italian heritage, has similar memories. He, too, from early childhood, woke on Sunday mornings to the smells of his mother's cooking. He, too, considered his mother's meatballs better than anybody else's, a test of loyalty in Italian families. After both our mothers had passed on, it was a long time before Sunday morning smells enticed my family out of bed. I tried, again and again, but couldn't get it right. My gravy was either too thin, or it was lumpy; my meatballs were sinkers. I was tempted to quit trying, but if I didn't preserve this tradition, who would? I'd remember things my mother had told me—basically the importance of using authentic Italian ingredients. She loved telling the story of how my brother's Irish wife used Kraft grated cheese in her meatballs instead of the Parmesan revered by Italian cooks and couldn't figure out why they didn't taste as good. "No wonder!" my mother huffed. I never forgot that lesson.

I also remembered her telling me when I was a child that I wasn't ready to take on this motherly task. I could see her still, standing at the stove, hair pulled back into a tight bun, a big, boxy apron tied around her ample form, working so lovingly to please her family. I wanted to do that for my family. *When would I be ready,* I wondered. I identified with the young Italian wife in the movie, "Prizzi's Honor," who was told, "Go home and practice your meatballs."

I did; and with practice, came success. I knew I was ready to fill the void left by our mothers the first time Phil came downstairs, followed his nose to the kitchen, took a deep breath, and said, "It smells like Sunday in here."

A Treat Mentality

I remember the year 2001 for two reasons, neither of them good. It was the year the World Trade Center came down, and the year something "suspicious" showed up on my annual mammogram.

The road to recovery started with a day-long series of tests which began at an ungodly hour, as most hospital procedures do. Phil and I, our footsteps echoing down the deserted corridor, shivered in the morning chill. Strong antiseptic smells assaulted my empty stomach. "You should have eaten something," I told him. "You don't have to fast."

"Don't worry about me, I'm not hungry."

Following the instructions we were given, we presented ourselves to reception promptly at 6 a.m. An orderly led me to a narrow, airless room smelling of other people's clothes. The walls were lined with lockers where I left my street clothes and put on a flimsy robe that wasn't designed to stay closed. Clutching it around my middle with both arms, I followed the orderly to the site of the first test.

After signing in and showing proof that I was indeed Catherine Fiorello, which I would do repeatedly during the day, I was led into a room with an ominous-looking, body-long tube. I lost my breath. *I can't put my head in that tube!* Sensing my panic, Phil took the technician aside. "My wife is very claustrophobic," he told her. "Will her head have to go through?"

The technician calmed his concerns, then walked me around the machine, explaining what would happen and how long it would take. "You can do it," she said. "I'll be right here with you the whole time; I'll talk you through." The results of the MRI confirmed the suspicions the mammogram had revealed. The next step would be a biopsy that would pinpoint the exact location of the tumor.

We each have our own way of coping with trauma. I find I can get through anything if I know there's a treat at the end of it. Phil calls this my treat mentality; he claims I choose my doctors based on their proximity to a French café or a pizzeria. He may be right. If I know I'm going to Delfina's for a slice after a doctor's visit, I endure the extraction of two tubes of blood and the indignity of the public weigh-in without complaint. This mentality that my husband derides came to my rescue at a time when I needed it most.

A date was set for the biopsy. Phil and I were to meet Amy at the medical center the morning of the test. After turning over the care of her children and dogs to friends, she would go through the day with us. It started in the surgeon's office, where I checked in to have the test. I sat in the waiting room, signing form after form declaring I would hold doctors and hospital blameless if, in the process of curing me they happened to kill me, when Amy came in. She was carrying a foil-wrapped package that looked like a casserole, but I dismissed that thought. Why would she bring a casserole to a surgeon's office? She went to the desk and said, "I'm here for my mother's biopsy. Would you keep this in your refrigerator until we leave?"

"What was that you left with the nurse?" I asked when she joined us.

"I made you an eggplant Parmigiana," she replied.

Of all the foods my mother cooked when I was growing up, eggplant Parmigiana was my favorite. Having worked my way through college, I hadn't had time to learn to cook. In the weeks before my wedding, I took a crash course in eggplant Parmigiana and would not have considered myself ready for marriage if I had failed. It's not a difficult dish to make; it just requires a lot of time and makes a mess of the kitchen, frying slice after slice of eggplant that's been coated with flour and dipped in beaten egg. In the process, the stove and counters are splattered with oil, the floor is sprinkled with flour, and the house, upstairs and down, smells of frying for days afterward. Over the years, it's become our family's feel-better, welcome home, holiday and special occasion dish and, as such, is worth every bit of the fuss.

161

Amy waited with her father as I was wheeled away to take the needle aspiration test that would pinpoint the exact location of the lump before the biopsy could proceed. Everything depended on the accuracy of this test. The biopsy that followed would be meaningless if the needles didn't direct the surgeon to the exact area from which to extract a tissue sample. I was instructed to lie perfectly still, take shallow breaths, and not react at all to the *pressure*—the universal doctor's term for pain. At one point, the *pressure* was excruciating but I dared not scream or even flinch, knowing that would throw the test off. I closed my eyes tightly and forced myself to think happy thoughts. That's when I remembered I was having eggplant Parmigiana for dinner that night. At once, I was in a better place, pain-free and delicious.

In-Sync

I had been retired for ten years when I got my last chance to be in-sync with the world I live in. We had moved to San Francisco from New York and I was desperately lonely. Everything was new and everyone was young and I was not. I would never fit in here. I longed for the porch in that suburb I was so anxious to leave. As I had always done in times of stress, I sought solace in my local bookstore. Two or three times a week, I sat in a bottle-green leather chair that wore the slits and stains of others who had needed the comfort of being there. It was next to a window that looked out on San Francisco Bay. With each visit, a feeling of well-being washed over me. I had a book in hand and a water view, who needed friends?

This bookstore filled all my needs. Some days my browsing brought me back to Left Bank Paris and I sat again at a sidewalk table at *Les Deux Magots* when two sparrows swooped down and made off with pretzels in their beaks. This being the Bay Area, home to Alice Waters, sustainable greenmarkets, and a restaurant for whatever your food preference, my foodie obsession was well fed in its cookbook section. I especially enjoyed watching the children in their corner nurturing what I hoped for their sake would become a lifelong reading addiction. Sitting on miniature stools, stretched out on the brightly colored alphabet mat, pulling books from the shelves at will, no one there to caution them, "Don't touch!" It was their place and they were free to touch and turn the pages and exclaim their delight when they found Waldo.

The store manager and I often chatted about what we were reading. She invited me to events where I met authors promoting their new books. One day, as I was checking out a purchase, she put a job application in my hand and invited me to join her staff. I accepted her offer and only later did I remember that she hadn't asked my age before making it, and I hadn't told her. It just wasn't relevant for either of us. She was looking for a reader and she knew she'd found one. What she didn't know at the time was, she had also found a writer. After a year on the job, it was my book that was being introduced at the store, I was the author the packed room had come to meet. When she offered me the job, she said, "We can only pay minimum wage." Something else she didn't know: I would have worked there without pay.

I had retired twice before and twice had succumbed to the pull back to a part of my life that I loved. But I knew this would be my last appearance in the workplace and I couldn't have asked for a better finale. Today's world is vastly different from the one I had graduated into so long ago, but here I was, late in life, working a part-time job in what may be the last bastion of humanity. I felt relevant, putting good books into the right hands, satisfying the mutual needs of my customers and myself.

Once again, I was the oldest member of the staff, but that was not an issue. My friend's mantra didn't apply here. There was no age box that would define me as unemployable. Being welcomed back into the workplace after a ten-year hiatus, knowing that I still had something to contribute, was a major turning point in making peace with my move. I was no longer in transit; I was home.

The Bread Is Warm

Sitting in the front row of the Commonwealth Club, nibbling samples of della Fattoria's Meyer Lemon-Rosemary country *boule*, Jenna and I were in our element. We had come to hear Kathleen Weber tell the story of how she had created the famous loaves in her farmhouse kitchen. One bite of her signature loaf and I had found myself in the flush of a new love. I ended my long-time romance with the renowned Acme Bakery whose herb-infused slabs and sourdough baguettes had sustained me since I arrived in San Francisco, and lost my heart to the wood-fired loaves baked on a farm in Petaluma.

Weber was invited to speak at the Club because della Fattoria had been nominated for a James Beard Award, the

Oscars of food accolades. When I called Jenna and asked her to join me, she immediately said "Count me in." I knew she would. She was weaned on the contentment derived from a simple slice of artisan bread spread with unadulterated butter, its every calorie in place. A high school student at the time, she was the youngest person in the audience. Young people, often not attuned to the nuances of bread, are insensitive to the glaring differences between the plastic-wrapped supermarket varieties and the artisan loaves our family travels all over the Bay Area to find. Baked the day we buy them, their seductive oven-fresh aromas entice us to start eating them on the way home.

We learned from Weber's talk that the bakery has a café on Main Street in Petaluma where the bread is served and sold. We had to be there. A call was made to Jenna's brother Joe, a full-time student at UC Davis in Sacramento and part-time bread-baking enthusiast. "I'll meet you there," he said. That Sunday, Joe drove south, the rest of the family drove north, and we rendezvoused at the café at noon.

The sandwich and salad menu was pure Alice Waters driven, California organic all the way. But we weren't there for healthy fare; we came for the bread and the butter-rich pastries. We ordered the Minimum Required Amount of lean and green, and devoured two baskets of pastries: plain croissants and *pain au chocolat,* cheese and raspberry Danish, apple braids and sticky buns. We bought Meyer Lemon-Rosemary *boules* to take home with us.

In my family, bread is the tie that binds us. If I leave a legacy at all, it will be that my children and grandchildren believe that bread is the warmest, kindest of foods. I've taught them well, and I taught them early. When Jenna wasn't much more than a toddler, with the tips of her fingers, she'd gently touch the bread in the basket that was brought to our table in a restaurant, a serious look on her face. If it wasn't cold, she would light up as she announced, "The bread is warm, Nana," our barometer for how good the meal that followed would be. She never outgrew the passion for bread that she was raised with. When she was a freshman in college, she took time out from studying for finals to email me, "Nana, did you know today is National Croissant Day?"

Sometimes, when I'm at a restaurant, I fantasize that Jenna is sitting down to a meal, too. When the bread arrives, she touches it. It's not warm. She turns to her Heavenly Host and says, "Dude—my Nana says the bread has to be warm. You better heat it before she gets here."

Requited Love

We all know what unrequited love is, it's one of the seven basic plots in literature, and in life. At some point, we have all loved someone who didn't love us back. I was seventeen, a junior in high school, too young to dwell on the pain of unrequited love. I had a life to prepare for. I put him out of my mind and moved on. Does it matter that I carried his picture in my wallet long after I graduated? That I will always remember his name?

Things got better. I went on to love one man and three dogs in my life; all of that love was requited. The first dog was mine by default. My brother Lou was in college at the time and his roommate bought a dog that came with prestigious credentials from the American Kennel Club. He also came with an incurable disease. The pet store owner replaced the sick dog with a healthy one that was not as expensive as the first, but he would not refund the difference in price; instead, he threw in another dog. My brother adopted the refund puppy, but wasn't allowed to keep it at school. He left it with us the next time he came home. By the time he was ready to reclaim it, that dog wasn't going to love anybody but me, and nobody loved him as much as I did. I named him Buddy because he had become my best friend. I was seven years old.

My mother, who had never allowed us to have pets, had agreed to only a temporary stay for the homeless puppy and couldn't wait for him to move out. She did not want an animal in her house. They were messy, they were noisy, they scared her. But when my brother came for his dog, she wouldn't let him take the puppy away from me, and he didn't fight for what was his. My mother was a strict disciplinarian, but she was capable of bending when the welfare of her child was at stake. She knew I needed that puppy and, want it or not, she would live with it, too.

Learning to live with a dog she didn't want wasn't easy for her. When the rest of the family went to school or work each morning, she was left alone with an animal she was afraid of. I lived in fear that Buddy would be gone when I got home after school. Their relationship improved when my mother had a severe gallbladder attack and was confined to her bed for a week. Buddy never left her side until one of us came home. Hostilities between the two ceased, détente was reached. To my enormous relief, Buddy was no longer at risk of eviction; he had secured his place in the family.

Buddy came to us with no expensive papers. We were never sure of his breed; it didn't matter. He was a tan and white mix of cocker spaniel and unqualified love. We both thrived in that love for eleven years. He awakened feelings in me that I would carry to future relationships, with people, as well as pets.

I was in college when his health took a severe turn. Nobody would tell me it was time to let him go. The decision to put him down had to be mine. My father drove us to the vet's but he did not come into the surgery. The doctor led Buddy and me to a private room and injected him with a drug that would take away his pain, and his life. In the end, it was just the two of us, as it always had been. I learned a devastating fact of life that day: Loss is the downside of love.

The second dog wasn't bought for me, either. I was married, I had two children and had not planned to add a dog to our family. I was summoned to the school psychiatrist's office when Amy was in second grade. She was having a problem that we needed to discuss. "Can you come in as soon as possible?" Nothing makes a mother feel so inadequate as a call from the school psychiatrist. I sat curled into a chair in her office, arms wrapped tensely around my waist, bracing for when she would pronounce me "bad mother." I was relieved to learn what the problem was: Amy was falling asleep in class. "Is anything going on at home that might explain this?" the psychiatrist asked. Indeed there was. "We can't get her to sleep at night," I replied. Long after she was put to bed, her light was on, she needed one more glass of water, another bedtime story; she had a litany of excuses for not closing her eyes. Phil and I moved upstairs to watch television after dinner so she wouldn't be alone on the second floor. Nothing worked; neither she nor we could soothe her bedtime anxieties. Nobody slept.

"She needs a dog," the shrink ordered. "And the dog has to sleep on the bed with her."

"We can't get a dog, my son is allergic to dog hair."

"Get a poodle, they have fur, and they don't shed."

That's how Beanie, a black miniature poodle came into my life. Amy chose her, named her, and claimed her, but from the beginning, the puppy wanted to be mine; she stuck to me like velcro. She was in my arms or at my feet throughout the day. She accompanied me as I drove around town on my errands; I took her everyplace dogs were allowed. She knew what her responsibility was and she didn't shirk it. At night, she hopped onto Amy's bed and cuddled with her, waiting for her breathing to become steady. When it did, she jumped off that bed and hopped onto mine, circling until she found just the right part of me to nestle into. Everybody slept.

Beanie was raised simultaneously with my children. When she joined the family, Bobby became the middle child, and I became the mediator in the rivalry between puppy and boy. The puppy ran off with the boy's matchbox cars, the boy pulled the puppy's tail. When one of them came running into the kitchen from the playroom crying or yelping, I knew the other was misbehaving.

Poodles have long lives. Beanie had enjoyed a healthy, playful life for sixteen years, when she began to decline. The signs were undeniable; I had seen them before. I tried not to notice, but I knew our time together was coming to an end. I told the family what nobody wanted to hear. "Not yet," they pleaded. I discussed it with the vet, who said, "You'll know when it's time." I worked not far from home and began coming home for lunch to check on her. One day, I let her out the kitchen door and, as I watched from the porch, she wobbled slowly across the grass, then one knee collapsed beneath her and she walked blindly into a tree. She let out an agonized yelp. It was time. I gathered her up gently and drove to the vet's office. We had a long, loving farewell. I will always be grateful for the sensitivity of the veterinarians who helped me through those difficult times. For many years, my dogs were part of their lives, too, but they did all they could to comfort me. I thought I was totally prepared for Beanie's departure, but I couldn't stop sobbing when it was over. "I didn't think I would cry," I told the doctor, "I knew it was coming."

"There is no preparation for that final goodbye," he told me.

I have learned from the death of loved ones, people and pets, that what the vet told me that day is true; we never are prepared for goodbye. Whether it's after a long illness or sudden, the loss is shattering. I announced to the family that there would be no more dogs. I would not go through the pain of putting another loved one down.

We had lived six months in our dog-free environment when Amy sat in the kitchen one day and declared that our house needed a dog. "It just doesn't seem like home without one." She spread newspaper classified pages across the table;

ads for kennels were circled in red. "Go find us another dog, please."

We found Danny, a few weeks' old apricot poodle who made the car trip home to his new life snuggled into my armpit, the beginning of another canine love affair. He soon became the spirited rascal who had no intention of filling his docile predecessor's place. He would define and claim his own place in the family. He took some getting used to, but when we did, we lived sixteen rowdy years with this loveable scamp. Phil, now retired, took over his care. He brushed him daily to prevent the knots in his fur that poodles are prone to. He saw that his water bowl was never empty. He bathed him in the same plastic tub I had bathed our babies in. Yet, whenever I came home, Danny's head was at the window waiting for me as my car pulled into the driveway. At the end of the day, he shared my special chair and slept on my side of the bed.

I owe an enormous debt to the dogs in my life. To Buddy who not only gave me unqualified love, but taught me how to return it. To my memories of Beanie and Danny yelping happily as they dashed through the first floor, circling the dining room table, tails wagging, ears flying—just because I was home from work. This went on for 32 years, the combined lives of our two poodles, one raised with the children, the other who kept our nest from being empty when they were gone.

When we were debating whether or not to move to San Francisco, Danny's health was declining rapidly; he had the same old-age ailments I now have. I knew he couldn't make the trip. I asked myself, could we make it without him? We had good reasons for leaving New York. We needed to live in a kinder climate as we aged, and we wanted to get to know the grandchildren we had seen so infrequently over the years. Should our needs come before Danny's? When we arranged for a good home for him, we finalized our plans. The woman in whose care we left him when we traveled had two young children. They loved him; she allowed him to sleep on their bed when he was there. She agreed to take him; her children were delighted and I was relieved. He would be happy there, I lied to myself. I am still haunted by that leave-taking. So attuned to my feelings, had he sensed my sadness as he climbed into their car that last day? Did he know the hug we shared would be our last?

In the end, I didn't have to put Danny down, but I will always feel I let him down by moving away when he needed me most. Mothering, in any genre, is an oxymoron—driven by love and wracked with guilt. It's more than ten years since we left New York; Danny is long gone. Still, I stop in my tracks when I meet an apricot poodle on the streets of San Francisco. I yearn to bend down, to stroke it, to say "I'm sorry."

The Unquilted Chair

I sent my Christmas cards out early that year. Among them was an annual catch-up note to my friend Priscilla. Priscilla and I had worked together in Manhattan before we both married and started families in distant cities. She was the department artist, the rest of us were writers. Born and raised in New England, she was the stable, steadfast anchor we all dumped our copy on much too close to deadline and who always managed to complete the graphics in time to meet it.

That was just her day job. The art she was passionate about happened away from the office, in her tiny apartment in Greenwich Village. Except for my Depression-scarred mother, I knew no one who could stretch a dollar as far as Priscilla. The major part of her salary paid for art supplies and she lived, with dignity and grace, on what was left.

Her gallery shows reflected her New England discipline. There were etchings of windswept landscapes and snow-heavy tree branches standing strong against the elements. But it was the subdued watercolors of her cherished wildflowers, lovingly transferred from memory to canvas, that best revealed the person inside the artist.

Like most of us, Priscilla planned to re-enter the workplace sometime down the line, but the birth of her son presented her with a more urgent mission. Andy was born severely disabled and was totally dependent on his parents who built a loving, caring life around him. I learned all this through our Christmas exchanges of more than twenty years. Priscilla would write of her son's frequent setbacks and his infrequent steps forward. I ached for my friend as I read, "Andy's seizures are not well controlled," and rejoiced the year she wrote, "Andy is 16 and likes his special school." In the beginning, I found it hard to write of my two children's growth, fearing it might pain her to hear of others' thriving kids. But she always asked about them. "Is Bobby in high school now?" "I expect Amy will be off to college soon." Ordinary parental exchanges, with an extraordinarily sad undercurrent.

Over the years, I reached a level of comfort with this, and also found it easier to ask about Andy. I came to understand that the most hurtful thing I could do would be to tiptoe around the world Priscilla lived in. When I got over that hurdle, I looked forward to Priscilla's note each Christmas and to writing her, guilt-free, at last. Throughout the years, whatever else was going on in her life, she continued her art.

Like Andy, art was her destiny, and life without either was unthinkable.

Priscilla's Christmas note came late the year I sent mine early. It was longer, and by far the saddest I had ever received from her. "Andy died in his sleep in August," she wrote. "He was only twenty-three, and happy and well the day before. It's been a terrible shock for us, but we are trying to cope and miss him dearly. He was the center of our lives for so long, and a sweet, loving person."

I needed to write a second note at once. But where would I find the words to console my friend when I was so overcome with grief myself? I couldn't help her accept her loss because I couldn't accept it. I decided that instead of a letter of condolence, I would write a thank-you note. I thanked her for sharing Andy with me for so many years. I told her that hearing about their life together had become an almost holy rite of my Christmas season, one that always set my straying values back on track. And this final news of him did it again.

Just before Priscilla's note arrived, I was getting ready to go to battle with the manager of a furniture store because I had ordered a couch and a chair with quilted upholstery, and had been delivered a quilted couch and an unquilted chair. After reading her note, I called the store and cancelled the complaint. "I can live with the unquilted chair," I said.

I continue to live with it. Whenever I find myself becoming unstrung by an issue of no real matter, sitting a few minutes in my unquilted chair helps me re-set my values. It is at once a symbol of sadness and of purpose, a comfort and a powerful reminder that life doesn't always play out as planned.

A World Without Why

Finding a new normal is difficult. I go along, fighting off the *Why?* in ways that have always helped me through life's traumas. I read. I write. I immerse myself in trying a new recipe, pretending Jenna is coming to dinner.

Jenna is my granddaughter. I no longer cook dinner for her because her life came to an abrupt end in a car crash when she was nineteen years old. I ask myself, over and over again, *Why did it happen?* I have had to accept the reality that there is no answer. I have to be able to live in a world without *Why?*

Our family, smaller now, has grown closer. We carry on, but we each have our dark moments when we live again the late-night phone call that changed our lives forever. We no longer celebrate holidays, we get through them. Adjusting to life without Jenna is painful; setting the table for five instead of six will always hurt. She is still an indispensable part of our lives. I don't think of her in the past tense; she continues to dwell in my present.

I still expect to hear her voice when the phone rings. "Hey Nana, it's Jenna Rose. Want to hang out today?" Hanging out with Jenna took many forms. We would check out a new café in North Beach. Or go to a talk at the Commonwealth Club. And book stores, we never passed one without stopping in to browse. The last time she was home from school, she said she wanted to read *All the Light We Cannot See*. I did, too. "Buy just one copy," she said. "You read it first, then send it to me and we'll talk about it the next time I'm home." I bought the book, read it, and sent it to her. We never had that book talk. Sometimes she came to the apartment just to read together, she stretched out on the couch, I settled into a comfortable chair, no conversation needed, no better way to spend a day. How will I fill those hours without her?

A grandmother's role in life is to pass her wisdom on to the young. The learning went both ways with Jenna and me. A conservationist from her earliest years, she taught me the importance of recycling plastic bags. She also taught me how to brush my teeth without wasting water. She was four years old and was on a visit to New York from her San Francisco home. The first night, when she was getting ready to brush her teeth at bedtime, she asked for a plastic cup. I watched as, standing on a stool to reach the sink, she poured water into the cup and turned off the faucet. She brushed, rinsed her mouth with the water in the cup, then dipped her brush in the remaining water

184

to clean it. Not a drop wasted. In his best professional script, Phil wrote "Jenna" and "Joe" on two plastic cups which were ready for them on future visits.

Even when she was young, Jenna had a presence. She knew who she was, she liked who she was. Her image of herself was not based on what she was wearing. She was a regular shopper at Goodwill, delighting in telling me the bargain prices she paid for "vintage" clothes. We had many discussions on the difference between clothes that are vintage and clothes that are just old. I lost every one; I was no match for her convictions.

Dressed in her good buys from Goodwill, she presented herself to the world as *Jenna Rose*. Her parents honored my mother by giving their daughter her name, and she wore it well. She always thought of herself as more than Jenna—she was Jenna Rose. Her signature, whether on her library card or her credit card, always included the Rose. For nineteen years, my mother lived on in her great-granddaughter.

Jenna's shopping philosophy, however, was the opposite of my mother's. When I was a girl, I had to outgrow or wear out an item before my mother would okay the purchase of another and I often returned home from shopping trips empty-handed. Not so with Jenna. When I looked longingly at a trinket or a kitchen gadget, then decide not to buy it because I didn't need it, Jenna would say, "If you love it, Nana, you don't have to need it." Everywhere in my apartment there are reminders of things of I didn't need, but Jenna said it was okay to buy.

On a visit to San Francisco when Jenna was six, Phil and I were invited to the local YMCA to watch her and Joe take a swimming lesson. The pool was full of children splashing about joyously but I spotted Jenna immediately. She was the one in the bright pink swim cap clinging to the side of the pool with both hands. I saw myself at her age, so afraid to let go and regretting it ever after. *Let go, Jenna!* I silently implored her. *Let go!*

Unlike me, Jenna did let go. I wonder now, did the tenacity with which she went on to face life start there? I've often wished I could emulate her resilience, but I can't. Thomas Wolfe couldn't either. In an extraordinarily poignant passage in *Look Homeward, Angel* he writes of his anguish when his brother Ben died at age 27: *I can believe in the nothingness of death, and of life after death. But who can believe in the nothingness of Ben?* It's been many years since I was first moved by that passage. Only now do I feel its full impact; now I, too, must learn to live with an unending absence.

I continue to go from sad to awed and back again as Jenna is remembered by so many in such loving ways. Friends gathered in Golden Gate Park where she volunteered for years, and planted a pink magnolia tree in her memory. We tamped the soil around its fragile roots, then sprinkled it with water and tears. A paver stone at the Fountain Plaza in the Great Meadow, donated by the National Parks Conservancy, acknowledges her work as an "Educator and Environmentalist."

I shudder to think how close we came to not moving to California. Had we not taken that risk so late in life, if there had not been more pros than cons on that yellow legal pad when we were debating the move, I would have missed the wonder of watching Jenna grow into the remarkable young woman she became.

I will live the rest of my life with my unanswered *Why?* Some days are easier than others. Then, without warning, it hits me all over again, and I want to shout to whoever is up there, *What were you thinking? How could you let this happen?* On those dark days, knowing that she lives on in the hearts of all who cherished her is not enough. I need to sit and read with her again. I need her to fill that empty chair at my table.

Uneasy In My Easy Chair

Chairs have always been essential props in my life. My first special chair was my father's, actually, a brown leather man-sized Morris Chair commandeered by my mother to help see me through a childhood illness. She tucked cushions alongside its arms and a pillow against its back, fussing until it was a perfect fit for my frail young body. The chair stood next to a sunny window in the dining room, where I could watch her budding hydrangea bushes grow in the garden, and she could watch over me as she toiled in the kitchen. That's where I got my first sense of the comfort a special chair provides. I was seven years old, and I never forgot it. As I passed from one stage to another in my life, I have sought and found a chair

189

that stood open-armed, ready to embrace me when I needed refuge from the world outside.

I've had special chairs at different times of my life, wherever I lived. The yellow chair in my suburban home was my sanctuary when I needed respite from the demands of young motherhood. It absorbed today's stress and restored my resolve to face the same anxieties tomorrow. This chair was indisputably mine. The green metal chairs in Paris parks were shared with dreamers the world over. They were always there when I returned, whether after months or years. I relied on them for the stamina I would need to visit again the sights that I never tire of in this city that I love. These chairs have had the easiest task of all—they simply make happy times more so. My current chair, purchased when we furnished our apartment in San Francisco, wasn't chosen for its style or color. The only requirement was that it be comfortable. There is no way the chair itself can compete with the view it looks out on. Outside my window, the Ferry Building's clock tower presides over San Francisco Bay, the flapping of its flag an indication of how windy the day. Behind the tower, the Bay Bridge is strung out in sections, its illuminated cables make nighttime magic. Between the tower and the bridge, the white wings of sailboats glide over the Bay.

I sit here now not because I am stressed or over-worked or multi-tasking has left me frazzled. I sit here now just because I am tired. I find I need to sit more at this time of life, to rest when nothing untoward has caused fatigue. My earlier chairs called to me at the end of the day; this chair beckons more frequently. When I was little and we went for Sunday afternoon drives, my father would sometimes pull to the side of the road, turn off the ignition, and announce, "I need to rest." Eleanor and I whispered quietly on the back seat as he dozed for fifteen or twenty minutes. He woke refreshed, and we continued our drive. I have not yet given in to the mid-day nap.

Though I've never allowed my advancing age to dictate what I can do and what I can't, I'm beginning to think in those terms now. This conflicts with the fact that I am still excited about life; I still delight in achievements, mine and those of others. I have not yet drawn the curtain on learning; I am still a classroom junkie. I am awed by a technology I don't understand but appreciate its effects on the world I live in, and can only imagine the monumental changes it will bring to a world I am no longer in. But the need for more rest, more often, is undeniable. This makes me uneasy in my easy chair.

An underlying need nudges at me. *Put your life in order,* it says. *Do not leave chaos behind for others to deal with.* I've started dispensing my personal treasures to those who I think would love them as I did. Letting go of things I've cherished is a source of serenity. Yet, paradoxically, this too makes me uneasy.

Lately, when I look at the view from this final chair, I have a different perspective on the Bay that I love. I see it as my final resting place, where I'll ride the gentle tides along its shore, then float out to sea to places I've never been. Though I couldn't swim in life, I will float fearlessly out of it.

Wellfleet

Last night I dreamt I went to Wellfleet again. In my dream, I pull into the parking lot at Newcomb Hollow Beach, which sits atop a solidified sand dune. I can't see the ocean yet, but I can smell its brine in the air; I can hear the waves rush boldly in, then slide back out to sea. I make my way from the car, my steps tentative because the dune is so steep that, until I get my first glimpse of the beach below, I fear I will drop off into space when I come to the edge. When the sand and the water come into view, I gasp, as thrilled as I was the first time I saw this breathtaking stretch of beach far below, the ebb and flow of the great Atlantic washing its shore. This is what brought me back all those years. This is what I dream about now. If Aladdin's genie granted me just one wish to go back in time, this is where I would go.

Wellfleet is a laid-back beach town on Cape Cod, just south of the land's end that is Provincetown, far from the madding crowds of Hyannis. Its casual lifestyle is a perfect fit for those who come to relax and revive in its sea and sand. We vacationed there when our children were at an age when you wish time would stand still and they would always be as safe and happy as they were then. Maybe that's the reason I yearn to be there again. We were all at a good time in our lives, our cocoon of safety not yet threatened by the world outside.

To get to the beach, we had to scramble down the dune, one arm loaded with chairs and towels, the other grasping the hand of a toddler. If I could go back today, I probably would no longer be able to descend that dune, and I know for certain that I couldn't make the steep climb back up. But I dream of the times I could, the times when we spread our blanket in the sand and secured its corners against the ocean breeze with the sneakers we had kicked off; when the children helped unfold our chairs and pop open the umbrella for Dad, no sun worshipper he, then scoured the shore for treasures that had washed in with the tide.

"Look, Mommy," six-year-old Amy says, showing me a shell with jewel-like sparkles on it. "I found a magic shell. I'll take it home." She drops it into the pail we had brought for such finds. Bobby, three, is more likely to carry home the sun-bleached shell of a sand crab, which I will meet again snuggled into his sock drawer on a bleak winter day and sigh with yearning for the beach it once crawled on. I sit at water's edge, taking deep breaths of the exhilarating air and exhaling my anxieties, as my husband and children run along the ridge of a dune, flying their kites above me.

On the way home from the beach, we stop at the Lobster Hut, a seafood shack at Wellfleet Harbor, home to a picturesque fleet of fishing boats where the day's catch is sold to vacationers waiting on the docks for their ship to come in. I am introduced to the lobster roll here, another enduring love I owe to Wellfleet. Glistening chunks of lobster bathed in butter are stuffed into a traditional New England roll, split open on top, and grilled. We line up at an outside window and place our order, adding corn on the cob to the rolls—and a hotdog, always a hotdog, for Amy. We take our seats inside at one of the long community tables covered in red-and-white plastic and wait for our number to be called. I've had lobster rolls in many places since then but none compare with those I had in Wellfleet, the lobster pulled out of the ocean that morning, eaten in a still-wet bathing suit and bare feet.

When the children were grown, Phil and I continued to go to Wellfleet, sometimes just for a weekend in the fall, by then our favorite season on the Cape. The summer vacationers were gone; the beach was ours for solitary walks along the shore between breaking waves on one side, soaring dunes on the other. Whenever we returned, whether it was months or years between visits, the beach, the sea, the dunes were in place, just as they were when I first fell in love with them. I am a strong believer in returning to the places you love.

One fall, the day before we were to drive to Massachusetts, a hurricane alert for the eastern seaboard predicted the coming storm would be one of the worst in years. The New England beach towns were directly in its path. We decided to go in spite of the warnings. When we reached our inn, we found the windows boarded; the outdoor furniture was being dragged into the barn by wind-beaten staff. The maples that lined the path to the door shuddered; their leaves, just yesterday the vibrant yellow of the season, curled inward.

"Good to have you back," the desk clerk greeted us. "The worst of the storm is still ahead; just stay away from the beach and you'll be safe."

We dropped our bags in our room and headed for the beach. We were relieved to see a few cars in the parking lot; we weren't the only ones throwing caution to the hurricane winds. The ocean's roar was threatening. We pushed open the doors of our car and moved slowly toward the edge of the dune, fighting a fierce wind that pushed us back. Clinging to each other, we made our descent to the beach and joined the others who had ignored all warnings to have this once-in-a-lifetime experience. I had never been at the mercy of an ocean so angry, never been tossed by a wind so violent. It seemed both wind and water were testing their might, and our resolve. But we stood firm at the shoreline, our band of adventurous strangers, feet dug deeply in the sand, arms tightly entwined, and held our ground. Finally, spent, we climbed the dune back to safety.

We ate chili by candlelight at the inn that night. It was the only item on the menu, cooked before the storm knocked out the utilities. It was a night we would always remember—the hot chili, the cozy glow, the pride we felt in having defied Nature's wrath and survived.

I dream of being on Cape Cod again, though I know I never will be. I live thousands of miles away from this place that I love. I am no longer a young wife, a young mother. I am no longer young. There is much to enjoy in my life here and now, and I am content. But in my dreams, I walk the beach at Wellfleet again.

Epilogue

Maya And Me

My granddaughter Leah's college paper, the catalyst for this book, has much in it that makes me content with the way I've lived my life. She identifies me as "a woman who has always kept her hand up." Seen through her eyes, I am a paragon of womanly achievement. Though I am not as exalted in my own eyes as I am in Leah's, I accept her sanguine assessment as something that comes with the territory. All her life she has looked at me through rose-colored glasses.

However, she may have overstepped even the bonds of love when she put my name and Maya Angelou's in the same sentence. In the first reference she tells of Angelou's fight to be hired as the first female African-American cable car conductor

201

in San Francisco. I can identify a bit with that. I had a similar struggle with agents who would not consider my work because I was not yet published, and with publishers who put my submissions directly on the slush pile because I didn't have an agent. We live in a world where nobody wants to take a chance on a first anything. So yes, both Angelou and I did have that hurdle to overcome.

It's Leah's second reference to Maya and me that makes me blush to read, and even more embarrassed to report. She writes:

> *Though Angelou and my grandmother faced different circumstances, both women stood for what they believed in and pushed against what was expected of them. Both women used the power of their voice and the strength of literature to inspire other women to do the same.*

When I move on from the discomfort of being placed in such lofty company, I admit that I'm more than a little pleased that Leah thinks of me in that way. Talking about my late-life move to San Francisco, she writes, "It's the land of the Beat Generation, of Haight-Ashbury, of flamboyance, exuberance, and liberation. It's the land where, at age 75, my grandmother jump-started her life."

Though I had always lived within conventional bounds, I did embrace this new *laissez-faire* lifestyle. But when Leah asks about my hopes for the future, I rat myself out again. I tell her that I sometimes long for the simpler, safer world I grew up in.

Acknowledgments

I was lucky to be born into the family portrayed in these pages. I tell their stories with love and gratitude. To my father, who encouraged my improbable dreams and my mother, who tempered them with a large dose of reality; to my sisters and brothers who nurtured and inspired me, most especially Eleanor, a main character in my stories and in my life.

To all my mother's sisters, those valiant aunts who struggled through the hardships of the Depression but sent their children out into the world remembering only the love, our bulwark later in life as we faced our own difficulties.

Immeasurable thanks to the members of my writers' workshop: Michael Gordon, Norma Kaufman, Marsha

Michaels, Sue Woods and Vivien Zielin. They not only critiqued my stories, they lived them with me, sharing my grief as well as my joy. There is no adequate way to thank them. And to Barbara Rose Brooker, our teacher, coach, cheerleader, who helped us find our voice. There would be no books for any of us without her. Thanks also to OLLI, the Osher Lifelong Learning Institute at San Francisco State University, where we found each other; and to Gwen Sanderson, director of the program, who makes all things possible.

A special thanks to my editor, Melissa Cistaro, whose caring guidance made the book so much more than it started out to be; and to Book Passage in San Francisco, my home away from home when I moved to California. I am fortunate to have the unflappable Cheryl McKeon, manager of this feisty bookstore, as a friend and an advocate. She cleared many paths for me on the road to publishing. I will always be indebted to Eve Tulipan, managing editor at Stein and Day Publishers, who taught me a valuable writing basic: If you can't find the right word, change the sentence. I have applied that mantra to other areas of my life, as well.

I have been lucky, too, in the friends who have shared my life: Ron Jin, bookseller extraordinaire, who encouraged me every step of the way; Mary Donahue and Warren Schloat, believers and mentors from the start; Cathie Gysel, Anita Huber and Elaine Nolan, my dear friends and "Bridge Ladies," first readers of many of these stories. There are no limits to the role my niece Debbie McNamara, the family historian, played in the creation of this book. When my memory faltered, she filled in the blanks.

I will always appreciate the warm welcome I received in San Francisco, a city that's a magnet for dreamers like me, and in its cafés that were my writers' retreats just a short walk from home.

Everlasting love and thanks to my children, and to their children; they give meaning to my life. I hope what they read in these pages helps give meaning to theirs. And to my husband, steadfast and patient, always there, for all of us.

Finally, love and gratitude to my awesome granddaughter Leah for asking the questions that prompted this long look back at my life.

CPSIA information can be obtained
at www.ICGtesting.com
Printed in the USA
BVHW03s1449110818
524223BV00001B/89/P